JOHN BUTE

JOHN BUTE

An Informal Portrait

EDITED BY

MALDWIN DRUMMOND

MICHAEL RUSSELL

© Contributors, as named, 1996

First published in Great Britain 1996
by Michael Russell (Publishing) Ltd
Wilby Hall, Wilby, Norwich, NR16 2JP

Typeset in Sabon by The Typesetting Bureau
Allen House, East Borough, Wimborne, Dorset
Printed and bound in Great Britain
by Biddles Ltd, Guildford and King's Lynn

Designed by Humphrey Stone

CONTENTS

FOREWORD

John was so well known to so many people but also so unknown in a myriad of ways, yet loved or respected or admired by all.

I wanted to have a little book which would surprise with undiscovered traits or recall others to make us smile or glow in the warmth of his memory. Maldwin Drummond kindly offered to edit this for me.

JENNIFER BUTE

ABOUT THE CONTRIBUTORS

[Dr] **R. G. W. Anderson** [MA, D.PHIL, FSA, FRSE], curator, historian of science and museum director, first worked at the Royal Scottish Museum in 1970. In 1984 he returned to Edinburgh and a year later became the first Director of the National Museums of Scotland. He is now Director of the British Museum.

Ian Archibald used to live on the Ayrshire coast opposite Mount Stuart. After war service in the King's African Rifles he spent ten years in the Malayan Police during the Emergency until independence curtailed his career. Thereafter he was engaged in charity work, principally fundraising for medical research, and is now retired.

Normile Elliot Baxter, sometime Scots Guards, member of Council National Trust for Scotland, and governor of Ludgrove Preparatory School, was previously engaged in the steel and oil industries.

Caroline Beaufort [The late Duchess of Beaufort] (1928–95) was a sister of the present Marquess of Bath. She married David Somerset in 1950, moving to Badminton when he succeeded as 11th Duke of Beaufort in 1984. She loved adventurous travel and she and the Butes went on several holidays in India and the Far East.

Robert W. Begg [CBE, MA, CA, D.UNIV] is a practising chartered accountant (and a practising painter). Interested in the arts and its institutions, he served as a governor of Glasgow School of Art, as a Trustee of the National Galleries of Scotland and as a member of the Museums and Galleries Commission, as well as on the Council of the Royal Glasgow Institute of the Fine Arts, the Executive of the National Trust for Scotland and the Court of the University of Glasgow.

Peregrine Bertie, a year older than John, is a cousin who spent some of the war years at Kames, at Ampleforth and in the Army with him.

Lester Borley [CBE, D. LITT, FRSGS] was Director of the National Trust for Scotland, after Jamie Stormonth Darling, under John's Presidency.

[Dr] **Deepak Chopra** was born and brought up in New Delhi, India. He attended the All India Institute of Medical Sciences and after graduating moved to the United States where he established the American Association of Ayurvedic Medicine. An international expert in mind/body medicine, he looked after John at his clinic near Boston March/April 1993.

John Cornforth has written about country houses and allied subjects for *Country Life* since 1961 and has been a member of National Trust Committees since 1965.

Ronnie Cramond [CBE, MA, FSA (SCOT)] is a Trustee of the National Museums of Scotland. He graduated as Senior Medallist in History at Edinburgh and worked in the Scottish Office until he resigned to become Deputy Chairman of the Highlands and Islands Development Board. He was for three years Chairman of the Scottish Museums Council and is now Chairman of the Strathclyde Greenbelt Committee.

[Lord] **Anthony Crichton-Stuart,** Head of the Old Master Paintings Department, Christie's New York, has worked for Christie's since 1987, first based in the London office and since 1991 in New York. He is a specialist in Dutch and Flemish seventeenth-century painting. He grew up at Mount Stuart and was educated at Ampleforth College and Durham University.

Henry Crichton-Stuart, John's first cousin, is the second son of Robert, who was the second son of the 4th Marquess. He has his own business in Edinburgh and lives in East Lothian.

[Major] **Michael Crichton-Stuart** [MC] (1915–81), John's second cousin, served in the Scots Guards 1938–48. Keeper of Falkland Palace, he was appointed National Trust for Scotland Deputy Keeper in 1952, and chaired the Executive Committee of the National Trust for Scotland from 1967 to 1969, succeeded by John.

Niall Crichton-Stuart, John's first cousin, was born on the Isle of Bute: a soldier (Scots Guards), member of the Queen's Body Guard for Scotland, Knight of the Sovereign Military Order of Malta. Chevalier du Wissam Alouite (Royaume du Maroc). He lives in London.

Tam Dalyell [Sir Tam Dalyell of the Binns, Bt], Labour MP for Linlithgow since 1962, first knew John as a teenager on holiday at Loch Boisdale. Kathleen and Tam Dalyell are National Trust for Scotland representatives at The Binns, the Dalyell family home since 1612. He had many contacts with John as Chairman of Council. Kathleen Dalyell worked as a member of the Historic Building Council throughout John's Chairmanship.

[Sir] **Philip Dowson** [CBE, PRA] is an architect and President of the Royal Academy of Arts. He received the Royal Gold Medal for Architecture in 1981. Architectural founder partner of Arup Associates, he has been a member of the Royal Fine Art Commission since 1970 and a Trustee of the Royal Botanic Gardens, Kew. He was a juror for the Burrell Museum competition in Glasgow and was chairman of the competition jury for the New Museum of Scotland, working closely with John when he was Chairman of the Trustees.

Maldwin Drummond [OBE, JP, DL, HON D.SC] met John first when he was at university. They shared a great interest in the countryside of Scotland, England and Wales. He was a Countryside Commissioner and presently is the Commodore of the Royal Yacht Squadron. While living at Wester Kames Castle on Bute, which he bought from John, he spent many days at sea with him on *King Duck*.

Johnny Dumfries, John's elder son, is a former professional racing driver.

James Dunbar-Nasmith [CBE], architect, Professor Emeritus, was member of the Historic Buildings Council for Scotland 1966–93.

[Sir] **Alastair Dunnett** [HON LLD, FRSA], formerly Editor of *The Scotsman*, and latterly Chairman of Thomson Scottish Petroleum, is a journalist, author and playwright. He served for seven years on the Council of the National Trust for Scotland.

[Professor] **Raymond Edwards** [OBE, LLD] was Principal of the Welsh College of Music and Drama from 1959 to 1984. The College was established in Cardiff Castle in 1949 and in 1973, through the munificence of John, moved into a purpose-built building in Bute Park, Cardiff. Dr Edwards is a well-known lecturer and adjudicator and President of the Drama Association of Wales.

Tom Errington, designer, *trompe l'oeil* artist, mural painter and gilder, was involved from 1988 for over five years in the restoration work at Mount Stuart. Particularly, he designed and painted the ceiling in Lady Bute's study; designed and painted the walls of the Horoscope Room as well as gilding the Conservatory doors and fireplace overmantel. In the summer of 1992 he started on the painted decoration in the Chapel, which he also designed.

[Sir] **Nicholas Fairbairn** [of Fordell] (1933–95) was QC (Scotland), FSA, Conservative MP for Perth and Kinross, author, forester, painter, poet, TV and radio broadcaster, journalist, dress-designer, landscape gardener, bon viveur, raconteur and wit. He served on the Historic Buildings Council for Scotland under John's Chairmanship, becoming Chairman on his retirement. He was also a Trustee of Scottish Museums from 1987.

Anna Fekete is a young Hungarian musician who has spent most of her life performing, recording and teaching music. John was one of the first people to understand her situation and to help her towards realising her dreams.

Martin Gardner trained in horticulture at the Royal Botanic Garden, Edinburgh and worked for thirteen years at Windsor Great Park. He is coordinator of the Conifer Conservation Programme based at RBG Edinburgh.

Stephen and **Lavinia Gibbs** have lived on Arran since 1972. They explored the west coast of Scotland with John and Jennifer on several occasions aboard *King Duck*, experiences – and on one or two occasions, escapades – which will never be forgotten. Stephen was John's junior partner in their attempts to try and make Isle of Arran Foods into a successful business – in vain, as it turned out – and both he and his wife have been strong supporters of the National Trust for Scotland over the years.

Jay L. Glaser [MD] is Associate Medical Director of the Maharishi Ayur-Veda Health Center in Lancaster, near Boston, where he looked after John in March/April 1993. He is engaged in clinical research on the application of Ayur-Veda to the treatment of chronic diseases, including cancer, neurological disorders and AIDS.

Bobby Gordon [BEM] worked for Bute Estate (for three Marquesses) from 1941, the last thirty years as head gamekeeper to John.

John Greenall, stockbroker and friend of John, regards himself as 'a naturalised Scot', having lived in Scotland for thirty-five years.

Donald Hardie [OBE, DL, FRSA], Major, Queen's Own Cameron Highlanders, has served as Director Bute Fabrics Ltd, Deputy Chairman Museum of Scotland's Patron's Council, and Director Scottish Division, Institute of Directors. He was co-owner with John of Wood and Hardie Ltd and is Session Clerk of Humbie Kirk.

Sally [Connally] **Hardie** [BA] is from Atlanta, Georgia, USA; member of the Council and Executive Committee of the National Trust for Scotland, member of the University Court, St Andrews, Trustee of the Robert T. Jones Trust, Chairman of the Lothian Committee the National Art Collections Fund.

Marshall J. Harris [DPA] was Scottish National Officer of United Nations Association for twenty-seven years; Director of Scottish Educational Trust for United Nations and International Affairs for five years.

Clare Henry, printmaker, broadcaster, exhibition curator and art critic of the *Herald* since 1980, was on the Art Committee of the National Trust for Scotland and has written extensively on the Butes' Dovecot Tapestry Workshop. She is a founder member and ex-Chairman of the Glasgow Print Studio, and oversaw Scotland's contribution to the Venice Biennale in 1990.

Antony Hornyold was at Ampleforth and Cambridge with John and remained a close friend.

Jocelyn Humfrey worked for John Bute at Recollections from 1988 until its closure in 1996. Previous to this she worked as a musical instrument expert for Sotheby's for a number of years and ran her own catering company to enable her to travel. She also worked in the interior decoration and graphic design trades. She is widely travelled in China, Thailand, Indonesia, Europe and the US, with interest in art, architecture, interior design and music.

[Professor] **Peter Jones** [FRSE, FRSA, FSA (SCOT)], Director of the Institute for Advanced Studies in the Humanities at the University of Edinburgh, has served as a Trustee of the National Museums of Scotland, first as a jury member, and now as Chairman of the Client Committee in succession to John.

Dick Kingzett, fine art dealer, served with the Welsh Guards from 1940 to 1946 and took part in the campaign in Italy. He joined Christie's in 1944, deserted them in 1950 for Agnew's where he still works in an enjoyably part-time capacity.

Alison Kinnaird [MA, FGE] is a harper and glass-engraver. She was involved with a number of projects for John, including an engraved screen for his office at Mount Stuart, and also panels for the door leading from the Horoscope Room into the Conservatory.

[Sir] **Fitzroy Maclean** [of Dunconnel, Bt, KT, CBE] is former Member of Parliament for Bute and North Ayrshire, and a well-known writer.

John McVey has been associated with the Marble Chapel at Mount

Stuart since 1951, first as an altar boy and later as the honorary sacristan. He is the nephew of the late John McVey, Head Gardener to the 4th, 5th and 6th Marquesses.

Mark Marlesford [Lord Marlesford, DL], parliamentary lobby correspondent, Countryside and Rural Development Commissioner, is now Chairman of the Council for the Protection of Rural England.

Hanne Mason was Personal Assistant to John from 1979 to 1993, and is now Administrator at Mount Stuart.

[Professor] **James J. More**, designer and educationalist, was Managing Director of the Edinburgh Tapestry Co. Ltd, under the Chairmanship of John from 1987 to 1993. He is currently Head of the Department of Design at the University of Northumbria at Newcastle and was awarded his Professorship in 1994.

John Mott [LVO], captain Royal Navy (retd), was for thirteen years Administrator at Culzean Castle and National Trust for Scotland Representative for South-West Scotland. He was much involved in the creation and development of Scotland's first country park at Culzean and the restoration of the castle.

Tom Parkinson [Thomas I. Parkinson, Jr, KM, LLB], a lawyer, is a member of Scottish Heritage USA who has been associated with Scottish interests for more than fifty years.

Alex Paulin [BA, CA], born 1930, was educated in Scotland and England, and served with John in the National Trust for Scotland between 1966 and 1992. Now retired, he lives in Kircudbrightshire.

Francesca Pelizzoli, illustrator, painter and photographer, was commissioned by John in 1991 to paint five murals at Mount Stuart in the Family Corridor.

Mary Pendreigh came to Bute as an evacuee when she was nine years old. She married a forester on the Bute Estate, started work at Mount Stuart in 1966, left in 1969 and returned in 1977, looking after the family's general well-being until her retirement in 1991.

She lived for a while in Scoulag Lodge (designed by Robert Weir Schultz) and lives now in Kerrycroy village.

Andrew Percy was born in Africa and moved to England when he was seven. He attended school near Brighton and then Eton. After his mother met John in 1974 he spent many of his holidays at Mount Stuart. He married in 1988 and he and his wife, LaNora, live in California with their two sons.

Diana Percy [BFA, MSC], younger daughter of Jennifer, completed a Fine Arts degree at the School of the Art Institute of Chicago. She later worked as a commercial pilot in Zimbabwe and Australia, has recently completed an MSc degree in Botany at the Royal Botanic Gardens, Edinburgh, and is at present working in Tanzania prior to moving to Australia to live.

Richard Percy, John's elder stepson, was born in South Africa and educated at Eton and Cape Town University. He is divorced, with two daughters, and lives in London.

David Perth [The Earl of Perth, PC] is a cousin of John and knew him from childhood. He was a Minister of State for Colonial Affairs, Chairman of the Reviewing Committee on the Export of Works of Art and a Trustee of the National Library of Scotland.

Jeremy Pilcher was at Cambridge with John. He was subsequently a banker at Hambros and with an American banking consortium. He is now occupied in literary research. He is a Trustee of the Elizabeth FitzRoy Homes.

Meredith Pilcher [FRSA] has published several books under the name Meredith Etherington-Smith, including biographies of Salvador Dali and Elinor Glyn. She is presently Editor of *Christie's International Magazine.*

[Father] **John Ramsay** served in the Scots Guards from 1944 to 1955. After studying in Rome for four years he was ordained in 1959; since when he has served in parishes in the Borders, Edinburgh and West Lothian.

Jorge Ross, Chilean financier, was educated at Ampleforth and the Massachusetts Institute of Technology. He has been active in inter-American relations for many years and in forest-related industries, and is a director of Simpson Paper Company (USA). He helped look after Bute lands and interests in Chile.

[The Hon. Sir] **Steven Runciman** [CH, C.LITT, FBA, FSA], historian of Byzantium and the Crusades, was a member of the Executive Committee of the National Trust for Scotland throughout the period of John's Chairmanship of the Committee and was the first Convener of the Curatorial Committee, which John set up.

Francis Russell is a director of Christie's. His *John, Third Earl of Bute: Patron and Collector* (forthcoming) was written at John's request as his contribution to the Roxburghe Club.

[Sir] **Houston Shaw-Stewart** [Bt, MC] lives at Ardgowan, Inverkip, a near neighbour across the water. He was a close friend and soulmate of John, with a shared scatological sense of humour. He married Lucinda in 1982.

Lucinda [Lady] **Shaw-Stewart**, formerly London representative of the National Trust for Scotland, a member of its Council and Executive, is now a Vice-President of the Trust and Convener of the Curatorial Committee. She is a Trustee of the Wallace Collection and the Burrell Collection.

Jimmy Shields, father of Billy, was formerly butler to the Dowager Marchioness of Bute (Eileen) at Dumfries House – and before that chauffeur to the 5th Marquess of Bute.

William (Billy) Shields has worked for the Bute family in various capacities since the age of fifteen. He became chauffeur, then butler, and is now ranger at Mount Stuart.

Robert H. Smith [CA], a Member of the Museums Advisory Board chaired by John and Founder Trustee and later Deputy Chairman of the Board of Trustees of the National Museums of Scotland, succeeded John as Chairman in 1993.

[Dom] **Alberic Stacpoole** [OSB, MC, MA, D.PHIL, FRHIST.S] is from a military family. After Ampleforth he was commissioned from Sandhurst into the Duke of Wellington's Regiment and fought in the last year of the Korean War. Joining 2 Para he was involved in Cyprus and the Suez operation. Becoming a monk at Ampleforth in 1960, he edited the *Ampleforth Journal*. He went to St Benet's Hall, Oxford in 1979, and is now a parish priest near his Abbey.

Gavin Stamp is an architectural historian who was asked by John to write up the work done by Robert Weir Schultz for his great-grandfather and grandfather. After moving from London to Glasgow in 1990 to teach at the Mackintosh School of Architecture, he founded the Alexander Thomson Society, which John supported and of which he was Patron.

[Sir] **Jamie Stormonth Darling** [CBE, MC] was appointed Chief Executive of The National Trust for Scotland, first as Secretary and Treasurer, upgraded to Director 1949, retiring in 1983. He served two Chairmen – Lord Wemyss for twenty years, and John for fourteen. He was subsequently apponted Vice-President Emeritus NTS. He serves on various trusts connected with conservation and the environment.

Euan Strathcona [Lord Strathcona and Mount Royal], a fellow Scottish landowner, shared common interests with John in Scottish Heritage, gardens and boats. A Government minister, he was active in the House of Lords speaking on Scottish affairs, defence, energy, housing and recreation.

Stewart Tod [DA (EDIN), FSA (SCOT), RIBA, FRIAS], architect and senior partner in an architectural firm practising throughout Scotland from an Edinburgh office, is from a family of architects going back three generations. A specialist in conservation work, mainly historic buildings and scheduled industrial sites, he is presently an executive member of the Association for the Protection of Rural Scotland and a general trustee of the Church of Scotland.

Rosemary Verey, garden designer, author and lecturer, had the pleasure of helping revitalise the potager at Mount Stuart.

Kay Watt, under the Chairmanship of the Hon. James Bruce and John, was among the founding members of the Scottish Committee of the Royal Society of Arts. She was also involved in a number of charity and business projects including a connection with the Edinburgh Tapestry Company. She is now manager for Scotland of Sight Savers International.

David Wemyss [The Earl of Wemyss (12th) and March (8th), KT] was Chairman of Council and President of the National Trust for Scotland, being succeeded in each office by John.

[Sir] **David Wilson** [FBS] was a member of the Museums Advisory Group and a founding Trustee of the National Museums of Scotland. An archaeologist, he was Director of the British Museum and is a Commissioner for English Heritage.

Susan Wraight [MA, RCA] is a carver whose work ranges from misericords for Winchester Cathedral to netsuke for a prince of the Japanese Imperial Family. Since 1985 she has divided her time between England, where much of her work is commissioned, and Australia, where she established a studio after marrying an Australian. She was commissioned to do the animal and bird carvings for the bed in the Horoscope Room.

OBITUARY

FROM THE AMPLEFORTH JOURNAL: ALBERIC STACPOOLE

Let us, with respect, turn at once to the name his friends, his family and some of his colleagues use – John Bute: he was a modern man and liked the economy of a name composed of but eight letters. But equally, let us establish the names that came upon him. His grandfather, the 4th Marquess, died on 25 April 1947, when John was just back at Ampleforth; and thereafter the courtesy title 'Earl of Dumfries' came to him. His first son, another John, was born on 26 April 1958, and so till now has lived with that title: when he went into motor racing he was known as 'Johnny Dumfries'. John also inherited when his father died on 14 August 1956, the accumulated titles thus: Earl of Windsor, Viscount Mountjoy, Baron Mount Stuart [of Wortley, Yorks], Baron Cardiff: all these of Great Britain. Viscount of Air and Lord Crichton of Sanquhar and Cumnock, Earl of Bute, Viscount Kingarth, Lord Mountstuart, Cumrae and Inchmarnock: all these only of Scotland. A Baronet of Nova Scotia, Hereditary Sheriff of Bute and Keeper of Rothesay Castle – all this a burden given by blood before John set forth into his own life. No wonder he lived his adolescence and earlier manhood rather shy and reluctant; he had too imposing an entrance.

John Bute's father had been at Downside and Christ Church, Oxford, but he sent his twin sons John and David, and the youngest, James, to Ampleforth and on to Trinity College, Cambridge. He had served in the Royal Navy, but all three sons went on to commissions in the Army. John in his turn sent his son and heir Johnny to Ampleforth (for one year), and Anthony also. From West Downs, the twins came to Ampleforth in April 1946, John to St Wilfrid's under the housemastership of Dom Columba Cary Elwes, and David to St Cuthbert's under the more experienced Dom Sebastian Lambert. David's house was close, inclined to field sports and evening rounders; whereas John's was consciously aesthetic and clever with books. For the twins, 1947 was deep into snow and struggle until Eastertide: it was the bleak year that the 4th Marquess of Bute, KT, and his wife both died. John became an earl that summer, with his own address: Kames Castle, Isle of Bute; and soon he was joined in his house by James. Contemporaries included Joe Wansbrough (now Dom Henry, Master of St Benet's Hall) and the Hon. Paddy Pakenham (son of a cabinet minister in the Attlee Government). They all shared as headmaster the illustrious Dom Valentine Paul Nevill, CBE (1924–54), who had initiated the house system in 1926, thereby bringing Ampleforth past Downside to the higher reaches of schooling.

Separation for the twins proved painful, but they both chose to go beagling on Wednesdays up on the moors, partly to compare notes about house and classroom in those strained wartime days, where both staff and food were rationed. Even parental visits proved rationable, for there seemingly was neither time nor petrol. Dame Augusta Mary came up, but her husband had to defend Scotland or reorder Germany after hostilities. The St Wilfrid's housemaster had the same memory of John as his contemporaries: that he was slight, polite, dapper and diminutive. Aware of a calling to future dignity, he developed style, a gentle reserve and a quiet desire to please.

Early days were conventional. For his National Service he went into the Scots Guards, becoming a lieutenant in the RARO. He went up to Trinity College, Cambridge (the largest of all Oxbridge colleges) to read history. There he attended lectures given by the architectural historian, Nikolaus Pevsner; and fostered an interest in art history. He was to inherit one of the finest private collections of paintings in Europe; and to manipulate them for interest or need of money, believing that collections in private hands should 'move a bit' in their owner's lifetime.

When in 1954 John and David, separated by a mere quarter of an hour at birth, came of age together, they were given the freedom of Rothesay; bonfires were burned in the hills and the tenantry was feasted at Mount Stuart. The following year John married Nicola Grace, daughter of Lieutenant-Commander W. B. C. Weld-Forester, CBE; and they had two sons, Johnny and Anthony, and two daughters, Sophia and Caroline, the younger of whom, Caroline, was killed in a motor accident in 1984. This long distressed her father. John's heir, Johnny Dumfries, won the 24 Hours of Le Mans in 1988 at the age of thirty. The Butes' marriage was dissolved in 1977; and John went on the next year to marry secondly Jennifer, daughter of J. B. Home-Rigg and former wife of Gerald Percy.

John's father died before he was fifty in August 1956, bequeathing to his first son a heavy debt of death duties. It was a stark awakening for a conventional young guardsman receiving unearned gifts from life. It was remarked of this that successive Scottish Secretaries of State became immediate beneficiaries. Finding it hard to translate his fortune into liquidity, John arranged the donation of his property in Charlotte Square, Edinburgh to the National Trust for Scotland in lieu of debt; No. 6 becoming at once the Scottish Secretary's official residence.

The twenty-three-year-old 6th Marquess of Bute quietly took upon himself what was expected, civic and public duties. For almost twenty years he served on Buteshire County Council. Becoming a Deputy Lieutenant in 1961, he became Lord Lieutenant of Bute for eight years, and a JP as well. In 1966 he took the Chairmanship of the Scottish Committee of Action Research for the Crippled Child, accepting the Presidency of this in 1968 for seven years. For four years after 1964, he chaired the Scottish Standing Committee for Voluntary International Aid. Glasgow University made him Hon. LLD in 1970. In 1990 he accepted the Lord Lieutenancy of Argyll and Bute. These were tasks befitting his station, rather than his character.

His wisdom was to choose a low profile, to operate from influence rather than from authority, to dovetail the clout and outreach of the many national enterprises and charities in which he had a hand. His historic name, his secure seat with its cultural collections, gave him what he needed without his need to insist. To be granted acceptance, he had only to be effective – keeping the age-old principle of nobility. He came to know that he could afford to be self-deprecating.

He began at home (where charity begins), as an exemplary countryman who entirely knew the island of his name and all who lived on it. In a newer, less isolated age he had to campaign against tenant desertion: this he did by setting out to win over the new tourist trade; and to make the next generation better housed. Thus estate workers were put into uniforms of lilac colour, the fleet of farm and utility vehicles being thus painted and with the estate logo put on all its doors. He furthered his localised industries, building upon his father's Bute Looms advancement of the cottage hand-woven fabrics tradition; and so he connected the localised skills with the market of fashion – including providing Paris and London *couture* with special lines redesigned to respond to their individual commissions.

Partly by taste, partly for tourism, John transformed his own home, Mount Stuart, into an extensive place of remarkable beauty. A natural gardener, he enjoyed recovering exotic and endangered species from South America and having them propagated. And withal he was ever modest about his works. Perhaps here we should turn to what his friend Sir Jamie Stormonth Darling wrote of him:

> No one can know the width and depth of his benefactions to national causes, to charities and enterprises and countless individuals. His compassion and enthusiasms were all cloaked in impenetrable reticence about his multifarious activities. . . . Like all the truly good, he sought only the truth in any matter . . . expressing his original and visionary ideas with economy and lucidity . . . and yet it was his humour that won all hearts.

Fondly, obituarists have compared John to a famous forebear. Francis Russell wrote:

> . . . he bore an uncanny likeness to his equally elegant predecessor, the 3rd Earl of Bute, Prime Minister in 1762–3. The resemblance went further (than sartorial). As the 3rd Earl had acquired pictures for himself and for the young King George III, so the 6th Marquess took a particular interest in Scottish pictures and galleries. . . . As his ancestor secured royal patronage for such painters as Ramsay and Zoffany, and such craftsmen as Vile, so John Bute patronised artists and craftsmen of today. . . . The 3rd Earl created the botanical gardens at Kew and developed the policies at Mount Stuart, the gardens of which have been transformed in recent years. . . .

And thus too for architecture, and completing modern changes at Mount Stuart. Such tastes ran in the blood.

[24]

John Bute's true calling became evident in 1969 in his mid-thirties, when he was offered the Chairmanship of the Executive Committee of the National Trust for Scotland and subsequently became Chairman of Council. It was a lively period, when membership of the Trust increased five-fold and the numbers of visitors to Trust properties at least doubled – how much that was due to a quarter of a century of Bute's leadership may be a guess. He certainly gained a reputation for businesslike tact; and he certainly earned his reputation as an equally effective Chairman during his five years (1983–88) of the Historic Buildings Council of Scotland. During 1984–91 he was Vice-President; and from 1991 till his death he was President of the National Trust for Scotland. At the last moment, as he was dying of cancer – so very bravely borne – he was appointed KBE (Queen's Birthday Honours, 12 June 1993) 'for services to the arts and heritage, and to public life in Scotland'. The Trust must have been the first cause of that appointment, made so sadly late that there was no hope of his going to his Queen to be dubbed and honoured; he died on 21 July at his island home. It was said that none who knew even a proportion of his public achievement could but feel that his KBE was both tardy and inadequate. Sir Jamie Stormonth Darling, who had worked for the National Trust for Scotland from 1949 to 1983, felt that the award 'cannot begin to express adequately the high esteem in which John was held by a whole host of witnesses. . . . '

In the Eighties (his last decade, his fifties), to add to his work with the Trust, John became both a Trustee of the National Galleries of Scotland (1980–87) and Chairman of Trustees of the National Museums of Scotland (1985–93), while continuing to chair the Historic Buildings Council. He was constantly spoken of as decisive, businesslike, adroit; while the depth of his pre-meeting homework continued to cause amazement. In Edinburgh, it was a time of major reconstruction in the arts, the leadership being shared by John Bute and Robert Anderson (now in the south on similar tasks), as chief of Scottish Museums. The task had been to amalgamate two main collections with five specialist museums into the National Museums of Scotland, a process completed in 1992–3 while John was in the early stages of his cancer. It was a fitting climax to his service to Scotland; and it was accomplished with none of the high dispute that dogged the same restructuring in England.

In April 1993 John Bute took his Edinburgh curtain-call at the laying if the Royal Scottish Museum's extension's foundation stone. He supported the Secretary of State at this last event, as he had done earlier. It was said that without John's drive – even while mortally ill – the project would have withered. Without a trace of self-pity, he made his round of final farewells. He knew sadness enough already, having lost both his brothers and one of his daughters before him. His mother was dying with him, a sorrow to both.

On 26 October they shared a single memorial service – 'The Marquess of Bute and Eileen Marchioness of Bute' – at the Guards Chapel in London. Johnny, son and grandson, read the lesson. Two addresses were given, by Maldwin Drummond (Commodore, Royal Yacht Squadron) and by Peregrine Bertie, a cousin and Ampleforth contemporary of John.

JOHN BUTE REMEMBERED

R. G. W. Anderson

I first met John Bute early in 1984 in a dismal, windowless room in New St Andrew's House, home of the Scottish Office in Edinburgh. I entered (I had applied for the Directorship of the Royal Scottish Museum) and was confronted by the usual array of subfusc interviewers, except for one, who was wearing a jaunty blazer with red trimmings and check trousers. It was, of course, John, who did not ask me much but whose questioning managed to be both languid and penetrating.

I got the job. Coming up to Edinburgh to be briefed by the then Director, Norman Tebble, I was told one of those 'good news – bad news' stories, this particular one about the magnificent midVictorian museum in Chambers Street. The good news was that enough money had been set aside by the Government for maintenance of the building. The bad news was that the roof was rotten throughout, and for the next decade would have to be systematically removed and rebuilt. This meant that nearly every gallery would have to be closed, one by one, and every display removed to safety while the work was going on.

For the first year of my Directorship, the roof programme was planned. Even more significantly, the National Heritage (Scotland) Bill made its way through Parliament which would take the Royal Scottish Museum out of the Scottish Office and join it with the National Museum of Antiquities of Scotland, under a new Board of Trustees. The Chairman was to be John Bute. A large party was arranged for the evening of 30 September 1985 in the glazed birdcage-like Main Hall of the museum. At midnight, George Younger, then Secretary of State for Scotland, proclaimed the birth of the National Museum of Scotland. He thereupon ceased to be my boss and John and his Board took his place.

A few months later there was no option but to close the Main

Hall: the roof rattled dreadfully during gales and occasionally a pane of glass would come crashing to the marble floor. We knew that it was essential to announce to the world the existence of the new museum during our first summer in 1986 with a major exhibition and yet most of the building would be inaccessible. But we doggedly continued to develop exhibition concepts and by the end of 1985 we knew what we wished to put on – an exhibition which would deal with Scots and their world-wide contributions to invention, manufacturing, trade, culture, sport and much else besides. An important aspect of this would be that it could involve every curatorial section of the museum and hence indicate the breadth of interests which the new organisation covered. But where would we mount this exhibition?

We approached the Royal Scottish Academy and explained our plight. The President, Anthony Wheeler, was understanding and helpful. We could borrow the Academy for our exhibition but there was a complication. The Summer Show would not end until a month before the start of the Edinburgh Festival, which was when we wanted our exhibition to be open. Everything which would be needed to transform a picture gallery into a museum space would have to be achieved in four weeks. This would have to include building cases, installing the exhibits and setting up the lighting. We knew at an early stage that there was not enough electricity available: a new power line would be needed which would tap into the main cable in Princes Street. There were many other complications which we foresaw and we knew that others would be identified as planning proceeded. We resolutely decided that caution was not the right attitude at this early point in the life of the National Museums of Scotland.

A few weeks later I was woken up early in a hotel room in Philadelphia by a telephone call from the Museums Administrator, Nigel Pittman. He had done his sums. Putting on the exhibition would be a financial risk. The only way to proceed would be to pare down other budgets and have confidence that the public would come in large numbers. Money might be saved by shutting the front part of the museum in Chambers Street for a few months – in any case there was little point in allowing in the public simply to view scaffolding. Sleepily I said that I still thought the exhibition was a risk worth taking, though we should consult our Chairman.

One Sunday morning in May, immediately I had returned, I found myself with Nigel Pittman and Robert Smith (then the Vice Chairman of Trustees) on the MacBrayne's ferry bound for Bute. At Mount Stuart we enjoyed an excellent lunch with John and his family before we got down to our discussions about the viability of 'The Enterprising Scot' (the putative exhibition had been so named). We repaired to John's study and Nigel, Robert and I presented our well-honed arguments about why we should proceed. Our presentation was quite long, I remember: the issues were many and various. We then noticed that John seemed to have nodded off to sleep. Was he still listening with his eyes closed? Should we wake him, if he was indeed asleep? We droned on, and at the climactic moment when we said that our arguments led us to believe we simply had to continue, John jerked himself into consciousness, said we were perfectly right, and that the exhibition was on.

So on 7 August 1986, after an amazingly rapid programme of installation master-minded by the curator David Clarke and designer James Simpson, 'The Enterprising Scot' was opened by Gus Macdonald in the Royal Scottish Academy. We knew from the immediate gripes which came from the expected sources and from carping letters emanating from the usual newspaper correspondents that the exhibition would be a certain success. The overall attendance was 52,361 by its close on 5 October.

The stresses and strains induced by the exhibition and the roof had not been the best way to spend our first year, but its by-product was the bonding of the Board of Trustees and museum staff. We knew that John Bute was going to be an ideal Chairman.

And so it turned out to be.

Ian Archibald

Duncan Guthrie, late founder and director of Action Research for the Crippled Child, was most fortunate to secure Lord Bute's acceptance of the Chairmanship of the charity's Scottish Committee, at that time composed of prominent persons whose participation was designed to enhance the Fund's status.

Lord Bute recognised that prestige would not of itself increase donations to the extent needed to finance major medical research projects, so began the retirement of members by mutual agreement and their replacement by selected chairmen of local committees representative of the various regions and whose committees were actively engaged in raising funds.

Lord Bute's position as leader soon became known to the public and was seen as a guarantee that Action Research was worthy of support. Staff were busy in finding, recruiting, and motivating people and progress towards national coverage was quickly apparent.

Annual income rose impressively and increased year by year as committees strove good-humouredly to outdo their neighbours. He would remark that the credit was due to the enthusiasm of volunteers, the majority of whom were housewives, and had little to do with his presence among us.

Expansion was not without problems, the great cities having to learn how to harness support commensurate with their size and potential. Edinburgh organised events to cater for the various sections of its population. 'Glasgow and the West of Scotland', a time-honoured but outmoded concept, had to divest itself of such territorial ambitions to enable Greenock, Hamilton, Irvine, Kilmarnock, Paisley and many others to raise funds under their own flags, which all did to superb effect. Both Edinburgh and Glasgow later overhauled competition and made very large donations.

Examples of outstanding achievement were many; one will suffice. Ardgay, a small village in Ross-shire, raised more per head of its population than anywhere else in the United Kingdom in the years 1975, '76 and '77.

A charity dependent on volunteers must take care not to alienate any part of its supportive constituency. Border disputes arose occasionally, as in olden times, but Lord Bute's charm and ability as conciliator ensured that these were resolved satisfactorily, and more remarkable still, that no supporter was lost to the cause. How he found time for close involvement remained a mystery to all of us. His was indeed exemplary leadership.

In line with rapidly increasing income there were exceptionally low overheads, a crucial consideration which he made a point of stressing at Annual Meetings for retaining and confirming public confidence.

His advice was greatly valued as a member of the Fund's Council from 1977 to 1989, since his views were reinforced by the practical experience of Scottish success.

Hundreds of active supporters gave their time and energy, thousands of people gave cash, and millions of pounds were awarded in grants to Scottish universities and hospitals. Lord Bute described the local committee members as the salt of the earth. They in turn, from Unst to Eyemouth, from Stornoway to Stranraer, thought him the finest Scotsman of his generation.

Normile Elliot Baxter

I first remember John in Egypt in 1953, shy, serious to the tasks in hand, a little perplexed, and quietly amused by a guardsman's daily round. We were soon thrown into Army-scale manoeuvres and John found himself 'accidentally' as second-in-command of a company. Doing a captain's job in most trying conditions, he returned acclaimed for his emergent authority, decisiveness, and indifference both to discomfort and to constant demands upon himself. I did not see him for another twenty years or more after those few months together.

Then I discovered the man John had become – his sensitivity, kindness his innermost being. In matters of import he was always circumspect and deeply considerate. To tread as he did in the sheer breadth of his involvements and interests is to accumulate great knowledge, and to think as he thought is to have vision transcending all boundaries.

John's wealth was never the scale of his inheritance, rather was it his enduring compassion. He chose truth and right, and he set himself great tasks, accomplishing all with distinction, gentleness and honour.

He was a complete person in his every act, tolerant with deep humility, and courageous beyond measure. His was a Christian sense of purpose and his mantle modesty – we may be sure such paths lead to heaven.

Caroline Beaufort

Alas, I saw all too little of John Bute. Living the other end of the British Isles to him, our paths did not cross nearly as often as I would have liked them to have done. It was on our travels that we met most often – and he was a *splendid* travelling companion; always very quiet but always ready to come forward when any difficulty arose. So often when one goes abroad one is ashamed of the way one's fellow countrymen behave, but with John I enjoyed reflected glory when he invariably behaved like the perfect English gentleman that he was.

In India, in particular, I was proud of him; he managed to combine gentleness with authority. Authority is something that I am singularly lacking in and therefore much admire. Once we went on a magical walking tour in Rajastan. I, being much less fit than most of the group, puffed and panted my way up the extremely steep hills. I was terrified of holding the others up, but he, who was managing with ease, used to say, 'Shall we all have a little rest?' – enabling me to recover my breath without embarrassment. When we eventually reached the fortress at the top, we found that the only entrance was through a twelve-foot-long drain. Two foot by one foot. I thought I would not be able to get through it but, thanks to his encouragement, I had a go and emerged triumphant the other side. He was the sort of person who, when one was in need of reassurance, had the ability to calm one, and somehow he was always there when he was needed. Since he died there have been many occasions when I have thought 'If only John were here!' How often his many friends must have reiterated this thought.

Robert W. Begg

The 6th Marquess of Bute, John Crichton-Stuart, inherited titles reaching back to the days when his forebears were the High Stewards of the Scottish kings: his title to act and speak for his country needed no democratic mandate, it was born with him.

John also fell heir to a tradition of collecting and connoisseurship and not just of the fine arts (he had a huge collection of Chilean

Mount Stuart with the 4th Marquess and Marchioness of Bute – John's grandparents.

The Earl and Countess of Dumfries holding the twins, Lord David Crichton-Stuart and Lord Cardiff; 1933.

His Master's Voice. John aged one, 1934.

John and twin David and baby brother James, 1939.

HON. JAMES CRICHTON-STUART
1 year.

HELIA WALKER
1 year.

LORD CARDIFF
3½ years.

HON. DAVID CRICHTON-STUART
3½ years.

ANDREW BERTIE
7 years.

IONE WALKER
2 years.

NINIAN CRICHTON-STUART
1 year.

PEREGRINE BERTIE
4½ years.

The three sons of the Earl and Countess of Dunfries and five of their first cousins, 1936.

John and twin David with their shotguns, 1947.

Port Said, 1952. John and Tim Boyd Wilson cleaning up litter, which became a lifelong obsession.

John with Antony Hornyold, 1949.

Portrait taken when John became Marquess of Bute, 1956.

Her Majesty The Queen – visit to Isle of Bute, 1958.

Klosters, 1960. With Houston Shaw-Stewart and Peregrine Bertie. Taken by Antony Hornyold.

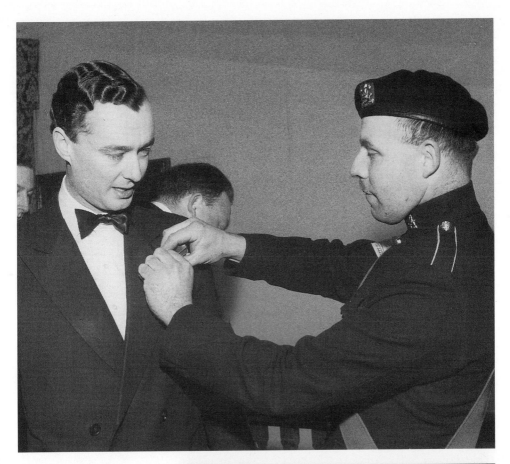

St David's Day, 1963,
Cardiff: Sergeant J. S. Curry
pins a leek on the Marquess
of Bute.

In Lord Lieutenant's uniform
in front of 'Raising of the
Standard' tapestry in
Rothesay Castle.

On the steps of 5 Charlotte Square with Jamie Stormonth Darling, early 1970s.

6 June 1974. Culzean Country Park Quinquennial Meeting. John with Ayr County Council Convener William Paterson and Provost Maisie Garven.

plants) but of active patronage of the arts. His great-grandfather donated to the University of Glasgow its splendiferous assembly hall. His family founded, and he revitalised, the Dovecot tapestries of the Edinburgh Weavers. With Jennifer, he restored the architecturally famous Rothesay Winter Garden Theatre; and he redeveloped the old cotton mill most sensitively to accommodate Bute Fabrics. In pursuit of good design he was a perfectionist. In many visits to the island I was aware that his staff referred to him among themselves as 'Lordie', but it was spoken with affection and pride.

Through my connection with the Hill House Trust I got involved with the Executive of the National Trust for Scotland. John Bute was its distinguished Chairman. His long service covered many of its significant developments. He was much concerned with Sir John Stirling Maxwell's family and William Burrell's Trustees in the transfer of land from Pollock Estate (over which the Trust had the restrictive agreement for its conservation) to secure the establishment of the Burrell Collection. He also had a great ambition to complement the number of stately homes in the North East of Scotland with some Glasgow vernacular property. This he realised brilliantly with the acquisition of Miss Toward's tenement flat in Buccleuch Street – complete with the bric-a-brac and ephemera of half a century: a veritable museum in itself. What a man, to see and enjoy this sort of balancing East and West, small and large! I never heard John discuss any proposal before the Trust except in the context of the widest vision of his country's wealth and needs.

As Chairman of the Board of Trustees of the National Galleries of Scotland, I asked John if he would be willing to serve. I then reported my 'catch' to the Scottish Office to be told in no uncertain terms that such invitations were the prerogative of the Secretary of State. (He later admitted we were lucky to get him.)

At a weekend teach-in which the Trustees organised after the arrival of Timothy Clifford as Director, John showed an unexpected grasp of all the many topics we discussed and also revealed his strong views on the respective roles of the Trustees and the Director on staff matters (a subject which was to lead, much later, to his resignation). His knowledge of Scottish history and genealogy combined with his sensitivity as a collector of pictures made him an ideal choice to lead the Committee of the Scottish Portrait

Gallery; and at Board meetings, and in between, he was a most valuable colleague.

It was no surprise when the Secretary of State appointed him to lead a working party on the amalgamation of the Royal Scottish Museum and the National Museum of Antiquities. This Museums Advisory Board is reputed to have been the happiest working group that any of its members had ever experienced. Its Report was a model of coverage of relevant and good ideas, of lucidity and of speed.

The Report was greatly praised but its expected progress to the shelf was resisted strenuously by John; and the implementation of the birth and successful development of the new National Museums of Scotland under his Chairmanship was pursued with such continuous and vigorous attack as to astonish ministers and senior officials, who gave way under the storm and marvelled that such a mild-seeming gentleman could have mustered such vehement advocacy. The Museums will remain perhaps the greatest of his many memorials.

How can one sum up this man? A gentleman he was and elegant and charming, an exemplar of perfect manners; approachable and kind yet shy and reserved except with friends or when duty demanded; of great qualities yet never putting down those less endowed; a man of human touch yet rare vision; of complete integrity. I miss him and I am not alone.

Peregrine Bertie

My earliest memories of John are at Dumfries House about 1936. They are of two little bumble bees with shocks of curly hair, one fair and one dark. This was the most obvious indication that John and David were dissimilar twins, although even then it was apparent that their natures were rather different; but what they had in common throughout their lives was their sense of fun, their humour and their kindness. When the war came we all went to Kames Castle at the north end of Bute, where we led a happy and carefree existence and, even though we still had the restrictions of nannies and the nursery, were able to run freely and where we all, John in particular, got to know and love the island so well. The great excitement of the week was taking the laundry to Mount Stuart, which meant a trip in that marvellous old Austin shooting brake which had had the words 'Bute Salvage Corps' written on the side, as it had been pressed into service for the war. There we used to be allowed to roam at will through the deserted house and the grounds, then rather sad, but now so lovingly brought back to life.

It was decided that something ought to be done about our education, so a governess was engaged and one day a gaunt and grey Belgian lady arrived in floods of tears off the boat as Belgium had just been invaded by Germany. With the unthinking cruelty of small children we immediately assumed she was a German spy and thought up endless traps to catch her in which John took a prominent and imaginative part. The result was that after a few weeks the wretched woman was put back on the boat, still in tears and on the verge of a nervous breakdown, and 'Madame' was replaced by Mrs Forbes from Rothesay, who managed very efficiently to keep us in order and to teach all five of us at different levels of education and give us the sound basic learning which enabled us later on to acquire what education we did.

It was then decided that the twins should go to school and they were sent to West Downs, which had been evacuated to Blair Atholl. One of the escapades they got involved in was entering the strong room at the castle which created quite a stir, and showed early the interest of the future great guardian of the National Heritage.

We were then all sent to Ampleforth and, although we were in different houses, seemed to stick together as a clan. The principal memories from that time were the holidays spent at Mount Stuart, where there were always so many things for young people to do and various hilarious and eventful journeys back to school.

By now, of course, we were starting to grow up and the time came for John to do his National Service in the Scots Guards. He could never be described as a person cut out to be a soldier, as he preferred his own discipline to the Army's and at that time was not well-known for his punctuality; but he got his commission and eventually joined the 1st Battalion in Port Said where our tent was one of the more popular centres for the sometimes riotous parties the young officers had.

John left the Army and, as might be expected, was in great demand by debutantes' mothers for their daughters; but he caused them endless grief and frustration as he was not very good then at answering letters, and telephone calls were often overlooked. There was one particular incident when he had arranged to meet one of these mothers at the St James's Club, completely forgetting that in those days ladies were not allowed into gentlemen's clubs. We had rather a jolly lunch which overran the time of the appointment and when we arrived at the club, which was then in Piccadilly, there was a very smartly dressed mother, who had been barred from the clubhouse, pacing up and down the pavement in a frenzy of rage and embarrassment, being ordered off the beat by the prostitutes who used to patrol Piccadilly in those days. John, with his consummate tact and charm, managed to defuse the situation and, needless to say, still got asked to her party.

These were happy, carefree days for John and he took good advantage of all that life had to offer, with enthusiasm. At the Coronation he was in the Abbey as a Gold Stick in Waiting (in charge of the ladies' loos) and then went up to Cambridge where he made many friends at a time when there was an exceptional vintage of talented and amusing people, many of whom were destined to play an important part in the world and who remained among his best friends for the rest of his life. The parties at the Pitt Club or his lodgings in Portugal Street were legendary, and the scenes were not very different to those depicted in *Brideshead Revisited* in pre-war Oxford.

The other big event in John's life at that time was the Coming of Age which brought out all the best in his character and which is described elsewhere in these pages. Also, there were the Christmas parties for the family at Mount Stuart which were always full of laughter, with things happening such as butter pats being flicked on a napkin onto the ceiling in the dining room, only to fall off at some later date to the consternation of anyone who might be on the receiving end, particularly nervous guests who had not been to Mount Stuart before.

Not long after this John embarked on marriage. This did not alter him very much, but sadly all too soon his father died and he found himself faced with the awesome burden of his inheritance. His salad days came to an end. It was then that the real strength of John's character became apparent. He coped, at this very early age, with all the difficulties and responsibilities and took his first steps into public life as others better qualified will tell.

John's outstanding qualities, which could be perceived from his earliest days, were his serenity and presence, coupled with his great kindness which was evidenced by so many generous acts, known and unknown, for which he wished no credit, and also his quiet, kindly sense of humour, combined with those exquisite good manners which are the true sign of a real aristocrat. In his quiet way he exercised profound influence on his family, the arts and Scotland and will be remembered for this by many.

Lester Borley

To me John was a modern man, whose sensitivity to the needs of so many important national bodies revealed a deep culture, which reflected of course the Bute family's traditional participation in the life of the communities with which it was associated. As a Welshman, I was well aware of the family interest which John sustained in Cardiff.

One of the illuminating moments for me was when Willie Cuthbert and I had to decide how to recognise John's achievement when he retired as Chairman of the National Trust for Scotland. I suggested to Willie that we should commission Alison Kinnaird to cut an appropriate piece of glass, because I knew that it would reflect his own tastes, which were always in advance of many of his contemporaries, and which showed the breadth of his culture. I know from visiting him frequently in London how much he supported the work of living artists and the pleasure he took in modern craftsmanship. It is this which I will always remember about him, and which is perhaps why so many things in Scotland today are better for the important, but often unobserved, part which he played in public life.

Deepak Chopra

Although I only met Lord Bute briefly, his inner strength was obvious in his demeanour and behaviour even in the midst of physical pain. He seemed to have transcended suffering.

[37]

John Cornforth

Alas, I did not know John well – indeed I always hoped that I would get to know him better through work, but mine has been mainly in England and for anyone with historical interests Berwick and Carlisle are frontier towns. However, from time to time work has taken me across the Border, and it was at a public meeting organised by the National Trust for Scotland in Edinburgh during the winter of 1974/75 about the threat to historic houses and collections posed by Wealth Tax and Capital Transfer Tax that I first met John, who had recently become Chairman of the NTS. After that our contacts usually arose over matters to do with curatorship in the NTS, in which he always encouraged me to say what I thought. And just occasionally I met him and Jennifer together. So although I saw little of him, I was deeply impressed by his rare ability to inspire and encourage; and I am sure that he had that effect on a great many of the people that he came across through his many activities. It was partly a matter of his highly developed Whig sense of giving, but also his intelligence and understanding, his willingness to master detail and his lightness of touch that made ordinary things special. If he was in the fortunate position to be independent, that enabled him to dedicate himself to what he believed in; also it enabled him to be open-minded and fair-minded. Also he had a strong visual sense that made him respond to the legacy of the past as well as encourage the work of designers, artists and craftsmen working today. Thus he was able to lead a multi-faced body like the NTS in a quite remarkable way. Later, when he became Chairman of the Historic Buildings Council for Scotland and of the National Museums of Scotland, he was able to steer all three complementary bodies forward in a way that always seemed excellent for Scotland.

In the thirty-odd years I have been involved with the National Trust, I have been aware of its debt to the handful of people with backgrounds and idealism similar to John Bute's, who led it from the mid 1930s to the 1970s; also I have been aware of how rare they have become in England. John Bute carried on their spirit into a younger generation in Scotland, and so it is a tragedy that he should have been prevented from continuing his work into the next century. When he died that tradition of service that he had inherited from his forebears seemed to flicker in the world of preservation on both sides of the Border.

When I first met John he had an elegance and a modern style that marked him out as being quite different from the tweedy folk assembled at the meeting, but also he had a shyness that was unexpected. He always retained his sense of style and he came to terms with his nervousness and also seemingly with the streak of melancholy that was part of his make-up. That I came to attribute to Jennifer's support and ability to take him out of himself. However, it is only very recently that I have come to realise that John's flowering as the inspiring leader of Scottish institutions coincided with his good fortune to meet Jennifer. Together they forged a partnership that enabled him to serve Scotland in the way he did.

Ronnie Cramond

When John was asked in 1984, by a previous Secretary of State for Scotland, to chair the Museums Advisory Board, he brought to that task a vision, a leadership and a courtesy which soon bound together a kenspeckle gallimaufry of talented individuals into a team whose personal friendship has continued to this day and who collectively mourn his passing but rejoice that they were privileged to know him and to assist the *common purpose*, but *uncommon ideal* which he identified: the provision of a worthy museum of Scotland's culture and heritage.

It is a measure of the man that, unusually for Royal Commissions and other prestigious Government committees, his Board produced, with remarkable expedition, a Report so cogent that its recommendations were not only accepted by Government but given statutory force with a celerity which astonished students of public administration.

So under the Natural Heritage (Scotland) Act, 1985, were constituted the National Museums of Scotland, under a body of Trustees headed, fittingly, by John Bute. From the beginning, the Trustees took as their primary aim John's vision of a new building which, for the first time, would properly display Scotland's unique collections of historic and cultural treasures and show, to

the people of Scotland and visitors alike, the surely dispropor-
tionate contribution which our small country has made to the
history of Europe, of the former Empire and indeed of the world.
Not just our own story, from geological time, through Pictish
symbol stones, the beautiful 'Work of Angels' in the so-called
Dark Ages, mediaeval thugs, Renaissance patrons of art and architecture, the whole, sometimes tragic, sometimes romantic, sometimes triumphant Stuart story, the Reformation, Calvinism and the
Covenanters, the French connection (e.g. the Lennoxlove toilet
service), the incredible flowering of multi-talented genius in the Age
of Enlightenment, the tragedy of the Clearances, the rise and fall of
the Industrial Revolution, Glasgow as the workshop of the world,
'Clyde-built' as a synonym for marine engineering excellence, our
role in two World Wars, right up to Silicon Glen and North Sea Oil.
But also the Scot abroad: students and soldiers; monks and mer-
cenaries, Gustavus Adolphus and Louis XI; all those explorers in
Africa and elsewhere; all those Governors General, Viceroys and
merchants who left their names or their legacies from the Mackenzie River to Hong Kong, where Jardine Matheson leads us back
to Lewis and Lews Castle built from the profits on opium and tea.
All those engineers, so that even now the engineer on the starship
Enterprise has to be called 'Scotty'!

This was his vision and he pursued it doggedly, until the
Secretary of State confirmed an earlier undertaking that Government resources would be made available and that work on the
building design and display briefs could begin in earnest.

The path was not always smooth. Indeed at one point, when
John suspected the Government of some dragging of feet, he wrote
so strong a letter to the then Secretary of State that the Permanent
Under Secretary of State, the top civil servant in the Scottish Office,
asked of one of the Trustees 'What's got into your Chairman? I've
never in my whole official career seen a letter in such terms sent to a
cabinet minister.'

But that is the advantage to an organisation of having a man like
Bute at its head. If a Government appoints to office a man of his
social and financial standing; his personal integrity and courage; his
vision, cultural patriotism and determination, they should not subsequently be surprised if he occasionally departs from his habitual
charming courtesy and speaks his mind when he feels it necessary.

It is so sad that John will not see the full fruition of his vision when the Museum of Scotland is completed in some three years' time. But it is good that he saw through to its successful conclusion the major international architectural competition for the new building, and was able, though by then grievously ill, to attend the ceremony, at which the Secretary of State inaugurated the contract for the building's foundations. No one who was present will forget the courageous humour of his speech that day.

The best memorial to such a man will be if Trustees and staff of the National Museums of Scotland redouble their efforts to fulfil his vision so that the people of Scotland will have, in 1998, an asset of truly international standing: an educational, social, cultural, historic and economic enrichment for themselves, their children and their visitors, including the Scottish diaspora.

Anthony Crichton-Stuart

My father was a 'gentleman' in the true sense of the word: both literal and metaphorical. I never once remember him raising his voice, let alone his hand. And yet he commanded, even from my earliest memories, a respect that verged on a sense of awe. His actions always seemed as if they stemmed from a deeply and carefully thought out process, and even his physical appearance was perfect. Indeed, looking through old photographs, I see how strikingly good-looking he was.

As a child, I remember going into his bedroom and watching him at his morning toilet (he would have laughed at the *double entendre* possible therein!): even today I can almost smell the aftershave and hair oil that he used, and can visualise him shaving. These simple acts struck me then as being somehow perfectly executed, and I remember aspiring to such mastery of ablution! However, he was always game for some rough and tumble horseplay with his children. My favourite trick was to snatch his handkerchief from his jacket pocket and run off with it in triumph (later in life I simply took to prodding it annoyingly into the depths of the pocket). This action was then normally followed by his dropping to his hands and knees and charging round the drawing room making ridiculous noises and pulling silly faces with me either in

[41]

hot pursuit or riding on his back mussing up his hair. As children we affectionately called him 'Mons', short for 'Monster', and he had the capacity for making us totally over-excited and hysterical with laughter.

Yet there was a paradox: although he was a very tactile man (all our lives we greeted him and said our goodbyes with a kiss on both cheeks), with an outwardly easy manner, he was also intensely shy and found proper communication with his loved ones hard. He could – and would – express himself freely and openly on paper, but person-to-person communication never came easily. Perhaps in this he was a slave to his upbringing and background, but I believe that it was a shackle throughout his life. I only ever heard his voice break with emotion once, and approval and disapproval alike were rarely communicated. This laconism was not just confined to others but included the way he presented himself, so that when I read his obituaries it was both with a mixture of deep pride and yet also sadness – sadness as not having known quite how much he had achieved in his all-too-short lifetime, or just how many people's lives he had touched. I should have liked to have had a chance to share some of those things with him.

I received so many letters of condolence when he died, in which the same words were repeated over and over again, such as 'kind', 'humour', 'gentle', 'modest', 'warm', 'caring', 'generous', and 'brave'. One person perhaps summed him up most succinctly when they wrote, 'I had known him since he became engaged to your mother, and I can honestly say that he was one of the most kindly and courteous persons that I have ever met. It was, however, his sense of humour and his interest in others that made him the person he was.' None of us who knew him will forget that twinkle in his eye or his peculiar brand of humour, so often expressed in his postcards. The last time I saw him alive (ironically, like my earliest memory, in his bedroom) the physical perfection had gone, his face ravaged by the effects of his cancer, but that same irrepressible twinkle was still there, undefeated.

He bore his terrible illness with a stoicism and bravery that was remarkable if not predictable, since he had displayed the same qualities throughout a life that had seen too many sadnesses and bereavements. I suppose that we all feel anger when someone so close to us dies prematurely – anger at their untimely removal from our lives, and anger at all the missed opportunities, things left unsaid, and unreconciled differences. The intensely private nature of my father perhaps over-exaggerated these gnawing regrets, but I feel sure that time will replace these negative feelings with only fond memories, and that my father's true spirit will remain with me, in Virgil's words and as inscribed on the monument in the grounds at Mount Stuart: 'So long as I am conscious and my spirit controls my limbs'. He *was* an unforgettable man.

Henry Crichton-Stuart

I have all my life been a passionate cricketer – player and watcher. When my grandparents were still alive and occupying Mount Stuart we spent much of the war and many happy holidays thereafter with John and his parents at Kames Castle. My first cricket lesson was from John, showing me batting techniques and a flowing off drive. I was probably about seven and he was still Lord Cardiff, a schoolboy of twelve. I was wildly impressed and the long passage within Kames made an excellent wicket.

So far as I know, the 6th Marquess of Bute and cricket were not exactly synonymous – in fact I never once saw or heard ever again anything to connect John even remotely with the sound of willow hitting leather. Indeed I suspect that were his Lordship to have entered a room to find the Test match playing on TV it would have been sharply switched off with an aristocratic grunt of displeasure.

Yet John may well be largely responsible for my love of the game – without question the indoor pitch at Kames and his elegant presence on it is an enduring happy memory.

Michael Crichton-Stuart

THE TWINS' COMING OF AGE: FEBRUARY 1954

Friday 26 February 1954 A lovely afternoon for the crossing from Wemyss Bay, a bright sun in a blue sky, and a fresh fall of snow on the Ayrshire hills and the Argyll mountains. On the boat were

Colum,[1] David and Ursula and their daughter Flora,[2] and Eileen's youngest brother John Forbes,[3] with a very pretty, fair Irish wife. It was mild and dead calm, but the latter clung grimly to the rail all the way, unsuccessfully determined to be sick.

Rothesay Pier, gateway to the Buteries, held a fleet of cars, from the inevitable very old Rolls to a Land Rover stuffed with young things from Mount Stuart, who had been touring the island when they saw the boat coming in. They had a quick quiet scoff before dashing off again. Elsie[4] was there to meet Colum and the Davids and take them to Ardencraig. I climbed into the Rolls with John Forbes and his wife and a mountain of luggage, very pre-war. So to Mount Stuart.

The graceless outcrop of red sandstone which serves to cover the guests' infiltration through the portals is calculated to awe, and does. But the winsome young man with long black hair and blue suit who answered the third tug at the bell failed to follow up the theme. With a nervous silent gesture he pointed to the model of Rothesay Castle to put our coats on. Then as we shot our cuffs and prepared to mount the marble stairs, he slunk off, beckoning, through a little door in the wall and down into the basement. The Forbeses, strangers in these parts, looked a little dazed when we were dumped without another word in the breakfast room. We were finishing our first cigarette when the young man returned and led us via the back stairs up to the drawing room. Here, among the Titians, was Eileen and some of the elders of the party.

It is probably best to give the cast at this point.

THE INNER FAMILY CIRCLE

The Marquess:	From lunch on only, entering and leaving always by the entrance next to the bar; fleshless, pale, haggard, harassed and hairy, ever kilted.
The Marchioness:	Constantly floating in and out, buxom, breezy and imperturbable.
Dumfries:	Always late on the scene, but playing the lead with reserved aplomb, good-looking and good-mannered.

1 Lord Colum Crichton-Stuart, brother of the 4th Marquess.
2 Lord and Lady David Stuart, brother of the 5th Marquess.
3 Brother of the 9th Earl of Granard.
4 Lady Colum Crichton-Stuart.

Little David:	Always looking thankful that he's not No.1; hard-drinking, shy and well-mannered.
The Lady Fiona:	The sister and youngest of the brood.

THE OUTER CIRCLE

Uncles David, Rhidian[5] and Jimmy[6] (Robert[7] had a bad tummy); Aunts Jean, Janet,[8] Ursula and Lilli;[9] and first cousins Peregrine,[10] Flora and Mary, [11] Ione and Helia [Stuart-Walker]. Forbeses – Col. F. (the Pasha), uncle to Eileen and John and his wife.

COLLATERALS

Me.

REVERENDS

The Bishop of Argyll and the Isles: a holy man and a man's man who can and does take his dram.

BROTHER DAVID

A budding Benedictine on hold from Louvain; a friend of Dumfries, in waiting as wanted on the Bishop. Piously pale, but a charmer undaunted by the glamour girls.

THE GLAMOUR GIRLS

Popping on and off the stage, single and in bunches: pretty, lively and decorative. Gore, Wyndham-Quin, Beddington, Grant, Smith-Bingham, and Weld-Forester, the current favourite.

YOUNG MALE SUPPORT

Jocelyn Stevens, tall, fair, rich and Aston-Martined; a smooth young man in a bow tie and a new Bentley; Alexander, a nice young soldier in a Jaguar; and one or two others, unmotorised.

THE FOREIGN ELEMENT

Count Revertera, Austrian, with his son, half Austrian, half Spanish. The count had piles for a start, and his son developed the collywobbles, so their appearance was not continuous. The Count

5 Another brother of the 5th Marquess.
6 Bertie, husband of Jean, sister of the 5th Marquess.
7 Another brother.
8 Wife of Robert.
9 Wife of Rhidian.
10 Bertie.
11 Sister of the 5th Marquess.

has a good sense of humour, but occasionally behaves foreign, as when he got pompous with the Bishop about the late Austrian Emperor and they had to be more or less forced apart, the Bishop muttering that he would like 'to tap the wee b . . . on the heid'. He is factor of the Guadacorte Estate, but by reason of his title was excluded from the Glenburn Mob.

THE GLENBURN MOB

A remarkable factorial-secretarial-solicitorial posse, housed out at the Glenburn, the monster hotel in Rothesay which belongs to the family firm. It included a strong Welsh contingent, Doolie (Miss Dowling, secretary to the late Bute) and Kit and Ian Pitman (the family solicitor).

OTHERS

In the big crowd scenes a number of others appeared, including a canon, a nannie, a French governess and so on. There was a recognisable basic domestic staff, but quite a number drifted about unknown even to the Marchioness. She admitted to meeting complete strangers in the back passages, but to have long ago given up wondering or worrying, even though they had got all the silver out. There were no visible signs of organisation, but meals got served (to never less than thirty when I was there), beds got made, and so on. It all seemed more or less miraculous.

There were only thirty-five to dinner the first night. I sat next door to Eileen and enjoyed myself as I always do with her. Through the gossip and girlish laughter neither the Bishop saying grace nor the piper with his subsequent blast got much of a hearing. Afterwards I was called from the drawing room by Dumfries to try and organise the Glamour Girls at country dancing. A feeble but gallant effort by the Marquess to do an Eightsome was a harrowing sight, mercifully short. Then it had to be explained to a lot of pouts that 'The Duke of Perth' didn't work on the pipes and so on, and after an hour or so as dancing master I sneaked off to the drawing room.

Beneath the arms of some far-distant collateral on a twig-tip of the family tree, embossed up in the south-east corner of the drawing room ceiling, and immediately overlooked by two life-size *Marriages of St Catherine* (Italian School), is a biggish marble table. This was the bar, and no nonsense. The time-wasting frill of decanting had been abandoned in favour of a more businesslike and uninhibiting row of bottles of whisky. The Glenburn Mob were in attendance, tightly massed round the dominating form of the Bishop, to whom they showed a due reverence and awe; not, as it turned out, so much for his cloth as for his whisky capacity. He had made a great name for himself in the war as a prisoner with the Highland Division in Germany, whence he had refused repatriation. He and Ian reminisced with an occasional Teutonic cry, while various Welshmen, evading beckoning wives, eased past them to the bar. Shortly before midnight the Mob were reluctantly urged into their long-awaiting cars, while the Bish helped himself to another, abetted by the Benedictine. Whether the latter's appearance was a bit of a reverent subtlety or not, his Lordship took a careful look at his watch and lowered it in one. It was one minute to midnight.

Saturday, 27 February D Day dawned bright and hard. There had been some confusion as to whether Mass was quarter *to* or *past* nine. On the way down at quarter to, the butler whom I met confirmed that it was definitely quarter past. I wandered out into the garden, and at ten past went into the Chapel. It was quite empty save for the Bishop, who was just finishing Mass, served by the Benedictine. Not too good.

The two heroes of the day made breakfast about ten, looking very un-Happy-Birthdayish. After, I went for a sharp walk with the Benedictine, then sat among desultory groups in the drawing room. Young David came in looking less heroic than ever, handed me a bit of notepaper and said morbidly, 'Do you think this will do?' As thanks for the Freedom of Rothesay it was a bit laconic – two sentences in fact; but for a shy No. 2 it did. I got an idea and wandered into the library next door. As I guessed, there was young Dumfries, with Good Evans, the secretary, in the throes of chain-smoking and composing the No. 1 speech of thanks. In fact it was good stuff and needed very little pulling into shape; but by the time it went on the typewriter we were due to leave for Rothesay in quarter of an hour. As we put the final touch a ghost came through the books in the wall, a skeleton croaking horribly through a huge moustache. The concealed library door made the apparition a hair-raiser; but when a sour voice added, 'Good God, the boy doesn't even answer me', I realised that the Marquess had not so much risen from the dead as surfaced two hours earlier than normal, to celebrate the joyous day, starting with 'Many happy returns'.

At 11.30 the Chosen Few (including me) assembled in the hall. All we wanted were the two Freedoms, who were both very late. However, we just got to the Town Hall at twelve. We entered by a side door, a notice and smell indicating the proximity of the Sanitary Inspector's office; then up a sort of annexe, whence the goats, including me, were sent on in to the packed Council Chamber. There were rows and rows of City Fathers and their consorts, with the Lord Lieutenant (Colom) and the Ardencraig bunch established in front. I found a seat next to Ian Pitman, whose crown was clotted with blood. The Freedom of Rothesay, one gathered, was already established at the Glenburn in the broadest sense.

In processed the robed and portly Provost, the bewigged Town Clerk, the skinny kilted Bute; Eileen, buxom and befurred, and the two boys, Dumfries kilted and (seemingly) confident, David trousered and reluctant. They sat and faced the throng, and the Provost opened up. It was all successfully decorous. The Provost's words were well chosen, and (for a Provost) short and to the point – the historic links between family and town and the roll of distinction to which they were added, the Duke of Windsor (ex of Rothesay), their father, some old Town Clerk, and now the twins, to make a majority of the Stuarts of Bute. As Dumfries signed the roll the photographers crept up and let off all their flashes just in front, but he managed somehow to look unconcerned; and then he stood up and spoke up, excellently and with barely a glance at his written piece. After him poor David, haltingly; and finally the Marquess to wind up, speaking emotionally of his emotion, but not too embarrassing; then round went the drinks – whisky, sherry, orange squash. Glasses were raised, refined little fingers quivering, and we toasted the twins and 'jolly-good-fellowed' them. After a decent interval we left the Council Chamber, nobs first, to watch from the portals as Mum and Dad and the twins drove off amid a large crowd 'happy-birthday-to-youing'.

On to the Glenburn, where the whole boiling lot were to be lunched by the Marquess. There was a high table, then a number of smaller ones presided over by members of the family, with the burghers and their ladies carefully interspersed among the family and the Glamour and the rest. I had table No. 5 with Helia Walker as my hostess; on my right a very refined councillor's wife, then the smooth Bentley boy from Mount Stuart; on left Sarah Gore and beyond her an extremely drunk Baillie, who rapidly resolved any fear of a dull lunch. Baillie Robertson, some years the wrong side of seventy, was apparently 'Father of the Council' – though his paternal propensities, if his style at lunch was anything to go by, were pretty unrestricted. From his spats to his white waistcoat and buttonhole he was a dandy. Sober he was obviously a character; plastered he was sensational. He had a double-track mind, women and wine of the country; and sitting next to Sarah with a large whisky in front of him, he was ebulliently aware that his interests were being well served, though he had quite forgotten what he was celebrating. With a less tough wench than Sarah, it would have been awkward. She was invited to Gretna Green about the fish course and to Monte Carlo (missing out Gretna) by 'The Queen'. My right-hand neighbour said coldly, 'You reely wouldn't think that Baillie Robertson's wife had died only three weeks ago.'

The whole party eventually dispersed ever so full of bonhomie into the winter sunshine, the Baillie being finally carried down the steps, an elegant but paralytic tailpiece. A shuttle service of cars took the Mount Stuart, Ardencraig and Glenburn Mobs to be photographed rather hangoverishly on the lawn at Mount Stuart. After that I had a little sleep till tea.

At six a pipe band with drums appeared, and played retreat on the lawn. It really *was* romantic, with the Chieftain Bute standing out in front, bonneted and cromached, and the twins on either side of him; the snow-capped hills of the mainland glowing faintly in the gloaming, the lights of Largs below, and then the sea, all a backcloth to the great lawn with its surrounding woods, as the flag was slowly hauled down. It was all very stirring, if parky. Even the GGs, huddled together for warmth, seemed impressed. It would have done the Welshmen good too, but the Mob were sleeping off their lunch at the Glenburn, preparatory to their dinner. This was to be for fifty-three, and scheduled for 7.45.

I was just finishing dressing for it when the lights failed. I groped my way downstairs thinking it was too good to be true. In the drawing room the fifty-three were assembling by the light of a couple of candles, and asking each other if it was sabotage and did they know that all the cooking was done on electricity? At the bar the Bishop had been joined by Canon McQueen of Rothesay, leaving even less room for the Welshmen to squeeze past. Around the room groups of the GGs were all dressed up and no one to see, and the posses of family said, 'Have you heard . . .?', Elsie said, '*Poor Eileen*', and Colum said, 'How extraordinary', and then the lights came on again.

Most of us went into dinner charged with at least two more cocktails than usual. Even the Mount Stuart dining room was a bit pushed for trough spaces for fifty-three. I sat between pretty Mrs John Forbes and the wife of the Dumfries House factor. We came to a working arrangement whereby they ate first while I sat back, and vice versa. It was a merciless squash, but great fun, and definitely unforgettable. In the centre of the table was the huge centre-piece of the two spies returning from the Promised Land, in solid silver, with a silver pole between them, from which hung real bunches of grapes that I last remember seeing at Bute's own Coming-of-Age. The Marquess and Marchioness sat in the middle of each side, like royalty, but not being able to see each other for grapes. Eventually Colum proposed the Queen with Lord Lieutenantly *je-ne-sais-quoi*, and the Marquess proposed the twins' health with a nice touch of sentiment, duly hurling his glass over his shoulder. Over the port a well-lit Welshman told me how popular my father was in Cardiff, 'as he was the first one of your bloody family who ever did a stroke of work'.

Thence to the bonfire. In cars went close members of the family or the owners (of the cars, I mean) and the GGs. The remainder, including the Glenburn Mob, the Bish and I, went in a bus. We seemed to travel for a longish time over naked rock before we eventually arrived at the top of some hill where we found the bonfire already lit. And there at the front of a large crowd stood young Dumfries looking very dashing and Bonnie-Prince-Charlie-ish, having started the thing. I escorted Doolie across the 100 yards of moor, and we all stood round and said 'ooh' or 'coo' till the butler came up to the Marchioness and said that the staff wanted to start dancing, so would the house party kindly scram and let them relax? The bus filled up, but we waited and waited and the Bishop started to get anxious as to whether we would get back to Mount Stuart before midnight. Then to our uninhibited fury we found the bus driver being Boy-Scoutish and helping to guide other motorists past his bus. A noisy démarche was made against this sort of charity at our expense, and we started to jolt off in the wrong direction, because that was the way we were pointing. The Bish and I, on the rear seat, got the impression after a time that we were being taken on an unwanted tour of his whole diocese, but we finally arrived at Mount Stuart just after 11.30. We found the *status quo* restored. The young (including Janet) danced; the relatives and dependants gossiped; and the pressure round the bar mounted, but I was beginning to develop the collywobbles and soon retired to bed. The last thing I remember hearing was Kit Pitman telling the Marquess (whom she was meeting for the first time) that his moustache was too big.

The pace was too much for my tummy. As the Bishop remarked, 'Some of us have been thrown a wee bit out of our normal routine.' I was not alone. (Uncle) David was soon down with a temperature; and Ione Walker; Rivertera's son was abed; and soon after I left the Benedictine went flat out with a full-blown heart attack. I personally gave up the unequal struggle after tea on Sunday, and retired to bed, only to be overwhelmed by kind callers. I was polite to my host when he woke me up at 11.30 at night to ask how I was; but when the Bish barged in at 12.30 a.m. overflowing with Quinquagesima charity, I only just managed to check a torrent of abuse. I could have tinkled his cymbal.

The junketings went on for a full week, but I left on the 7.45 a.m boat on Tuesday, feeling that duty had been done. At the tenants' beano Dumfries had again distinguished himself, and according to reports went on doing so for the rest of the week.

Niall Crichton-Stuart

It is almost impossible to describe John, as he was all things to all people. He was so incredibly intelligent and serene, yet kind, calm, thoughtful and loving. He always went out of his way to help others.

I remember, as a very young man, going with my father (Rhidian) to Bute to shoot grouse. It was the normal shooting party arrangement, arriving on a Friday and leaving on the afternoon ferry on the following Monday. The party was all family and all male, and I was the youngest by many years. David (Blackface), John's twin brother, always took a perverse pleasure in teasing me, and all others, relentlessly going on much like a terrier – never letting go.

On Saturday, on preparing to move to the moor and having drawn our numbers, I found to my horror that Blackface was to be in the next-door butt – this always meant trouble. I was not in the least surprised when Blackface informed me that he would be poaching all my birds, which he duly did! At lunch, in the Black Maria, John insisted on my sitting next to him. It was during a noisy and excellent lunch that a plot was hatched by John that would turn the tables on Blackface and give me immense pleasure. As we prepared for the afternoon drives, John rearranged the numbering in such a way that Blackface was always in between John and me. For those who remember Blackface, the inevitable explosion was wonderful to perceive as John and I went on to poach all Blackface's birds throughout the rest of the day.

The remainder of the weekend was a great success, and although the teasing continued, my protector, John, was always there.

Tam Dalyell

Not a soul who was present in the magnificent exhibition hall of the Royal Scottish Museum in Edinburgh on the occasion, in April, of the laying of the foundation stone of the new extension in Chambers Street, will erase from their memory the piquant nature of the ceremony. The Secretary of State for Scotland, Ian Lang, mounted the podium, and made a felicitous speech. Then the Marquess of Bute, Chairman of the Trustees of the National Museums of Scotland, took his place. His face and neck swathed in plaster, his voice, so authoritative in a panoply of official meetings, now distorted, he embarked on an excellent oration. That everyone invited knew he was in the last stages of cancer appeared to worry him not a bit. Conversing with everybody afterwards, there was not a trace of self-pity. It was a courageous and supremely dignified curtain call.

But then John Bute was courageous and dignified. And, without

[52]

his drive, in the face of incipient illness, the Museum Extension Project would have withered.

In the second half of the century, when the notion of public service is somehow going out of fashion, Bute was one of the aristocrats who stuck to the age-old tradition whereby those who inherited wealth believed that privilege brought with it responsibilities to the nation or their local community. Gaining publicity for good works, still less himself, was not at all Bute's style. Ridiculous gestures or posturings by organisations with which he was connected were out. He preferred to operate with a low profile. If criticism were to be levelled, it would have to be that he played his cards very close to his chest, and did not always inform his committee members of the options before they were presented with a *fait accompli*.

For sixteen critical years in the history of the National Trust for Scotland, Bute was Chairman of the Council and Chairman of the Executive Committee. By the nature of our job, MPs become connoisseurs of chairmanship, and as a five-year member of the large and unwieldy Council, I rated Bute extremely skilful at exploiting his diffident charm to get his own way. Sir Jamie Stormonth Darling, the former Director of the Trust, than whom no one saw Bute at closer quarters, says 'I cannot find enough superlatives to do him justice.'

Other experienced members of the Executive have used words such as 'adroit', 'businesslike', and above all 'decisive', to describe his work in committee. During his time at the helm, the membership of the National Trust for Scotland increased nearly fivefold. The number of visitors to properties also doubled over the same period to just under 2 million a year. It is a widely held view among the Trust's staff that Lord Bute deserves his share of the credit for these achievements, and for the fact that the Scottish Trust, albeit smaller, did not seem to become embroiled in the kind of embarrassing high-profile disputes which have plagued the English National Trust.

Between 1983 and 1988 Bute was Chairman of the Historic Buildings Council of Scotland. Justifiably, he was considered very effective, and my wife, along with other members of the Council in a position to know, admired the depth of his homework before meetings. We encouraged him to participate in the House of Lords

– but this he eschewed on the grounds that he did not enjoy part-time responsibilities, and that the Lords was 'not my scene'.

Secretaries of State for Scotland in the House of Commons have every reason to be grateful to him. At considerable personal sacrifice, he conveyed the centre of the north side of Charlotte Square to the National Trust. The headquarters are at No. 5. No. 6 is now Bute House, the official residence of the Scottish Secretary. And No. 7 has become the Georgian House, a big attraction to foreign visitors to Edinburgh New Town, with a flat above for the use of the Moderator of the General Assembly of the Church of Scotland.

Bute's good works were not confined to the Heritage. For a quarter of a century from 1966 he chaired the Scottish Committee of the National Fund for Research into Crippling Diseases. About his personal life, he was adamantly reticent, but there were a number of sadnesses, including the untimely death of a beloved daughter. I suspect his melancholy in middle age owed much to his private life. But marriage to Jennifer Percy, an enterprising wine merchant in her own right, brought him much happiness, and a valued relationship with South Africa on which his views were for tolerance and understanding.

Philip Dowson

John had a love of art and architecture and it was in this way that I came to know him, but it was not until he asked me to advise on an international architectural competition for the New Museum of Scotland, and to chair the Panel of Assessors, and subsequently to serve on the Client Committee responsible for its construction, that I came to know him well. I recognised very quickly that John civilised everything he touched, and brought to the most vexing and difficult issues a pre-eminent human dimension. This always made shared responsibilities and hard work with him such fun. Large undertakings are never easily won, and early on John was presented with both financial and, particularly, political difficulties, which required decisions of great courage on his part. Behind high aspirations and visions, there always lurks a shadow of Icarus.

We set as early a start to the construction of the New Museum of

Scotland as possible, and so divided it into two contracts. The turning of the first sod by John, on the first contract, driving an excavator shortly before he died, was a wonderful day and a celebration of his achievement, and launched an enterprise of great importance to Edinburgh and Scotland. This splendid legacy will embrace so much of art, architecture, design, and history, that during his lifetime were his abiding interests.

Perhaps one of the most vivid memories I have of John was his handling of what, by any standards, was an extremely difficult press conference, to announce the winner of the architectural competition, just two hours after Prince Charles had resigned as Patron. It left me with the impression of a friendly knock-up at tennis on a sunny Sunday afternoon. Wit, good nature, perception, irony, and unquestioned integrity – it was all there, and John at his very best.

Maldwin Drummond

ADDRESS IN THE GUARDS' CHAPEL,
TUESDAY 26 OCTOBER 1993

I first met John on the water. The mist of years is shrouding memory of this first encounter. We went on a Thames River steamer, chartered for the evening, I believe, by Simon Sainsbury. John must have been about twenty-one and I a year older. I think he was then at Trinity, Cambridge. He cut a slight, shy, upright, polished figure, beautifully dressed and easy to spot, not because of his clothes, but by the way he moved. He seemed to glide slowly through the crowd, who were pressed together in pleasure, without touching anyone. It was his way then and for evermore. This aura of detached remoteness, more often the province of saints and kings, was his most striking quality. Even when young he appeared austere, but that feeling was constantly softened by his infectious humour.

He would have been fresh out of the Scots Guards and about to make his mark on life. Lord Dunraven, the great sailor, who challenged for the America's Cup with his *Valkyries*, used to recall that in his early days he had to choose between the violin string and the tarry rope and had chosen the latter.

John arrived at the bottom of the ladder of his choice in the same way that he moved. He knew what was expected of him and that exactly coincided with what he wanted to do. He developed three skills at an early age, which provided the driving power of his achievement – his quick and appreciative eye, his ability to persuade, lead and to organise, and his close identity with Scotland's history, wedded to the need to encourage art and design.

John seems to have been a mix of two of his forebears, the 3rd and 4th Marquesses, with a green flourish from the 3rd Earl.

The 3rd Earl, with the widowed Princess Augusta, Princess of Wales, created Kew Gardens in the middle of the eighteenth century, and was, to all intents and purposes, the first Director. John similarly had a close identity with the Royal Botanic Gardens Edinburgh and his fascination with plants, no doubt coming too from his mother, and his sense of place, brought about the revival of the garden and grounds at Mount Stuart. This renewal was among his most recent achievements, much encouraged by Jennifer, with her marvellous enthusiasm and energy.

John's love of landscape was put to good service as a member of the Countryside Commission for Scotland, from 1970 to 1978, and was tested with the Oil Development Council from 1973 to 1978, when great steel and concrete monsters were built in unlikely and beautiful places in the North Sea Oil rush of that time.

John's great love was for buildings. He had a zest for decoration much in line with his great-grandfather, the 3rd Marquess. Indeed, the 3rd Marquess had acted on his own as a National Trust for Scotland and Wales, restoring and rebuilding Rothesay, Falkland Palace, the Old Place at Mochrum, Cardiff Castle and Castell Coch. The names run off the tongue; exclamation marks in a catalogue of restoration and re-creation. His grandfather was similarly driven and helped found the National Trust and the National Monuments Record, both for Scotland.

If genes could be marked by the stonemason's chisel and the painter's brush, John had them so decorated.

There is no doubt that among his many successes, his time with the National Trust for Scotland may be seen as a golden age. The Trust was recognised simply as the best organised and most effective conservation body in Britain under his chairmanship.

I remember his advocacy of the Little Houses Improvement Scheme in Fife and Dunkeld that started in 1960. We were standing by the fireplace in the lower drawing room at Mount Stuart. As usual, there were many gathered there before lunch, mostly the family, but a sprinkling of those whose friendship and expertise he valued. The family had a special place. His admiration for Johnny's brilliant achievement in his chosen field delighted him. The fire flickered, warmth and the sound of voices filled the room.

I asked him about the Little Houses Scheme. He looked up and I could see light in his eyes. If there was any distraction, it disappeared. He did not raise his voice, his evangelism was of the quiet kind, often speckled with a memory which tickled him. He promised details, a pledge he always remembered with a handwritten card.

So this idea took root, south, in Hampshire and some forty buildings and structures there have been conserved by a rolling fund and the scheme has spread country wide.

John passed on a similar trust when he let me have Wester Kames. 'I want someone to love it,' he said simply. I had said that I was looking for a building of architectural value and note that perhaps passed just below the horizon of the National Trust's own attentions. He sent me a note or two. One was a disused inn, once a laird's house in Drummond country, and the other a particularly interesting, post fortified house, overlooking Gruinard Bay, Wester Ross.

'Don't be seen', he urged, 'when looking at that one, for the owner has built a new bungalow just behind and wants to clear the view.'

Well, it was pouring with rain when I reached the end of the road. I decided upon a beach approach, a sort of crouched run and crawl, but only had an orange sailing jacket to keep out the weather. Remembering John's plea, I discarded this and reached the house unseen and soaking. The place was still furnished, the windows open, and the wind blew through streaming the ragged curtains out on the lee side – a heartrending example of neglect for such an interesting structure in a superb setting. The thought though of such a neighbour, happily, as it turned out, defeated the idea!

We should celebrate John's sense of humour and his ability to mimic. On the tenth anniversary of the National Trust's involvement with Culzean, there was a party in the boathouse constructed and clad by Lord Ailsa in beaten out tar barrels. They resounded to John's impersonation of the principal guest, the redoubtable Willie Ross, to the obvious delight of the original, who then endeavoured to return the compliment.

As Chairman of the Historic Buildings Council for Scotland John showed an unmatched care for the past but a strong eye for the future. He put his energies behind the new extension to the Museum of Scotland in Edinburgh, won by Benson and Forsyth with a Corbusian design. This drive was no better exemplified than on his own beloved island, with his creation of the internationally regarded Bute Fabrics.

John's attention to detail is celebrated in this little story. *King Duck*, his beautifully kept, Thorneycroft-designed, 1930 motor yacht, was chartered by a celebrated conservationist, keen to make the acquaintance of every puffin, guillemot and fulmar off Scotland's west coast. *King Duck*'s exhausted skipper, Jock McArthur, was heard to exclaim, 'Why cannot he behave like a gentleman, like Lord Bute, and retire to his cabin and study his agricultural returns?'

King Duck was in his thoughts a week before he died. Jim Mackenzie, the joiner and craftsman at Mount Stuart, remembers being there when John was working at a table in the conservatory. The table was unsteady and John had been looking for the cause. Jim glanced underneath and spotted the trouble. He would take it to the workshop.

'Don't worry,' John replied, giving the table another wobble, 'it's just like *King Duck*.'

For all his similarity with his forebears, there has been no one like John.

Johnny Dumfries

My father, John Bute, represented many different things to different people. As a result of the wide spectrum of activities of his working life, and the execution of his duties – as he saw them – he came into contact with a great many people. Those who met him were frequently left with a strong impression of his ability to communicate his kindness, his gentle charm and sense of humour, and his integrity. Myself and other members of the family would often find ourselves in conversation with strangers who, having met my father, would praise these attributes unashamedly. After his death, Sophie, Anthony and I received a flood of sympathetic letters in which numerous superlatives were used to describe his character and to praise his life's work.

From early childhood we were aware of the almost awe-inspiring effect which our father had on others. This imbued us all with a great admiration for him, a degree of admiration which I now believe stood in the way of a more open and honest relationship with those close to him. And because he was aware of the effect he had on others, it enabled him to create barriers which could be used to avoid dealing with contentious or emotionally loaded situations. For an acquaintance or business colleague this may have been of no consequence but as one of his children it mattered enormously to me. Of course, I accept my share of the blame for an inability to break down these barriers, and I will always regret not ever, once, having had the kind of conversation which I yearned for with my father. It is almost unbelievable that we continued this charade for thirty-five years.

On reflection, I am not surprised that my father's character developed in this way. Although outwardly happy, he had endured many difficulties in his lifetime. Brought up in a hopelessly repressed Catholic environment, reminiscent of the era of Victorian restraint of his great-grandfather, he was to suffer many bereavements and considerable sorrow. After a long period of illness, his own father died of cancer in 1956, leaving his son – barely out of his teens and with little experience of life – as head of the family, and with responsibility for the family and their business interests. His marriage to my mother, Nicola, failed and they eventually divorced after a long and traumatic separation. He lost both of his brothers before either of them had reached fifty years of age. But undoubtedly the cruellest blow was the loss of one of my beautiful sisters, Caroline, in a car accident in 1984. So excessive was my father's control over his emotions that he was unable to weep in front of the rest of his family even in this his darkest hour. In this respect it was my grandmother Eileen who was my father's chief counsel and source of emotional support. He would invariably stay overnight with her in Ayrshire on his return from business in other parts of Scotland. She was a woman with a powerful personality whom we all loved, and she too commanded an awe-inspiring level of respect from others.

The facets of my father's working life were rich in diversity: a land owner, businessman, National Trust for Scotland chairman, conservationist, patron of the arts, lord lieutenant, JP – the list is endless. He was fortunate insofar as some of these activities were also his passions. I once asked him what career he would have chosen if his life had not been so pre-ordained. After thinking for a short while he replied, 'An artist.' He truly loved the arts and had a very keen eye for classical and contemporary architecture. Evidence of this was his devotion to and involvement in establishing the Museum of Scotland, a project which he stubbornly backed practically until the day he died, in spite of narrow-minded opposition by a few renowned critics of modern architecture. The museum will be built and will stand as a symbol of his commitment to progress.

A considerable amount of time and energy was spent renovating his Victorian home so that its outrageous beauty could be preserved for 'future generations' – as he would have put it. In the course of the renovation work at Mount Stuart he employed many young artists and crafts people to complete parts of the building which were left unfinished in 1900, on the death of his great-grandfather. Apart from the work he commissioned, he also developed and incorporated some of his own ideas into the project.

The renovations at Mount Stuart were of course part of a larger, more ambitious plan. The house, policies and entire estate were to be vested in a charitable trust, the principal objective of which was to 'preserve Mount Stuart House, policies and estate as an integral unit'. This was one of his dreams, a dream which he saw become a reality (the trust was founded in 1989), but sadly his premature death deprived him of witnessing the public opening of the house in 1994. In hindsight, I think he would have found it difficult to cope with thousands of people invading his home for six months of the year. However, his vision was clear and his dream to create continuity in parallel with new opportunities is now being realised by us, his children.

Although he was an able public speaker, my father was not one to babble in conversation; his words were always carefully chosen. He had a great interest in the English language and was always looking up the meaning of words, which he would then use in conversation. He derived great pleasure from using a new word, the meaning of which no one had the slightest idea, and, waiting for the inevitable questions, would eventually supply the answer to his riddle.

As a young boy, I once asked him what work I should do when I grew up. His reply is imprinted on my memory: 'I don't mind what you do, just make sure you do it properly.' A philosophy which I admire and have tried to adhere to, although I remember thinking at the time that it would have made my life easier if he'd simply told me to become a train driver! Nevertheless, his comment set a precedent in our relationship, it was taken for granted that he, as head of the family, looked after family business, and that I was free to pursue my own life. This freedom was a great gift and was a mark of his unselfish and generous nature. It was for him a personal sacrifice as he relinquished a means of support which might otherwise have been available. As a result his working life was more isolated and lonely. And more recently, in 1991, after he was diagnosed with cancer, I informed my father that I had retired as a professional driver and that I wanted to help him with the administration of business matters. By that time it was understandably hard for him to relinquish control of an organisation which he had guided for nearly forty years and, thinking about it now, it seems to me that my offer was almost futile.

My father bore his illness with extraordinary courage. His cancer was both severe and visible, and attacked his mouth, face and throat, and even though the disease ravaged his good looks, impaired his speech and made it difficult for him to eat, it never bowed his spirit. He continued to work and on occasions would still speak in public. In 1992 I accompanied him to the Bute Shinty Club in Rothesay. The club has frequently been helped by the Bute estate, and for many years my father and members of the club enjoyed a close friendship. The occasion was the opening of a new club house, the timber for which had been supplied by the estate. It was a low-key event and my father was relaxed in the knowledge that he was among friends. Witnessing him speak was a very moving experience, bearing in mind that after his operation he required speech therapy to relearn the pronunciation of words. The room became totally silent so that he could be heard, and he soon had our friends laughing because, as usual, his words were warm and humorous. As I surveyed the assembled faces, I realised how well-loved my father was on the island.

Intimate moments were few and far between in our relationship. Towards the end of my racing career, despite earning considerable sums of money, I got into financial difficulties. I decided to visit my father in Scotland to seek his help. We were alone together and I explained the situation, we discussed it at length and he agreed to help me out. I remember feeling relaxed and sensed that he shared my mood. I itched to move onto other more personal matters, but as usual the invisible barrier was in place. At the end of the evening I said to my father that I regretted having to ask for his help, adding that 'I just got myself in the shit.' He smiled and replied that we all get ourselves into the shit from time to time. His relaxed attitude and understanding filled me with warmth. His unselfishness was one of the many reasons why my father was so well-loved by every-one who knew him. He was an exceptionally reasonable and under-standing person and I loved him a great deal.

James Dunbar-Nasmith

My first encounter with John Bute must have been when he was in his twenties. I was sailing in a regatta at Rothesay and a number of us – a large number – were asked to lunch at Mount Stuart. I was more interested in seeing the house, about which I had heard much, than meeting the owner, of whom I knew nothing. The magnificent luncheon was announced by an elderly butler who then walked out of the room backwards and I found myself wondering how such a young man would cope with life in such unusual circumstances. My great good fortune was in being allowed to see, over the next thirty years, exactly how he put it all to such good use.

It was not just that John used his privileges in the service of others, he used his time and his talents in the same cause. He seemed shy and I suspect that he did not find the exposure that his responsibilities brought him either easy or welcome. His modesty was genuine to the point of diffidence, but beneath it lay a steely determination to pursue anything about which he was certain. When he became Chairman of the Historic Buildings Council, I had expected him to be well informed about Scotland's old buildings, which he was. I had not expected how well briefed he would make himself about every case that came to the Council – a briefing which included not only the building but the owner, the finance and the function. During this period my friendship with and admiration for him grew spontaneously and, although he usually knew more than I about the topics we discussed, he always made one feel intelligent and erudite. It was through this interchange that I came to appreciate his unique quality as a patron of art and architecture. In everything he undertook, the quality of design was of paramount importance to him. Bute Fabrics, The Edinburgh Tapestry Co., his completion of Mount Stuart – and particularly the small alterations he made to it – were of remarkable excellence. He once chaired an architectural jury on which I served to select a design for a new building in an area of great natural beauty. Not only did he identify immediately the one design which was worthy of such a site, but patiently and logically persuaded the other members of the jury to his view. The ability to identify the potential of one imaginative scheme among scores of predictable ones is rare indeed. To achieve agreement on the matter comes near to genius.

Alastair Dunnett

It seems strange and sad to inhabit still a Scotland where there is no John Bute. He was everywhere, touching all our lives at every point, and invariably featuring in aspects which meant much to the status and future of his native country. In that he followed a great family tradition, for they had been around for all these centuries. Like so many others, I knew him as a colleague in things that were good for Scotland, and in many of these he had of course emerged as the natural leader.

My first intimate contact with him might be the occasion when I took my part in a minor logistic rescue operation. It was the time when I was a virtual Orcadian for some years, and he was cruising these islands in his fine motor yacht *King Duck*, of which more later. I encountered him somewhere in Kirkwall, and he told me that he and his lady needed to get south sooner than even that smart little vessel could make it. At that time I had an aircraft at my disposal, and was to travel south on that very day. So I picked them up at a secluded port somewhere in mainland Orkney, and we had a congenial flight to Edinburgh.

The reference to *King Duck* brings recollections of another ploy. In 1934 Seumas Adam and I had made a canoe journey round the west coast, and sixty years later it occurred to me that it would be suitable to cover the same ground again, this time in comfort and dripping with nostalgia. John chartered *King Duck* to me, and Seumas and I set out with our wives to do the thing in luxury, accompanied by one of my sons, as well as the designer Robbie McLean, a great companion of the canoe days. It went well.

There were many ventures with the National Trust for Scotland, including the unforgettable Meteor cruises, led or deputy-led by Dorothy and me, and supported by executives of such varying skills as deployed by Jamie Stormonth Darling, Donald Erskine, Isabel McClearie, John Forgie and many another.

I heard John give many extempore speeches, always kindly and compassionate and mindful of who should be thanked and for what. There was another side, however, to this articulate skill. When I was president of the Saints and Sinners Club of Scotland I had him attend one of our annual lunches to respond to the toast of the Guests. It was a revelation of advanced scatology, almost drowned in the telling by sustained laughter. He told stories and made allusions of a medieval character, which seemed to hint at some kind of family tradition of his kingly forefolk – the sort of discourse that must have set many a royal table in a roar. From such a mild man it was hard to believe, and dearly welcome.

There was a time when he showed me round the Dovecot tapestry undertaking which he had under his wing. Fifty years before I had doted on the Bute tapestries when they were exhibited in Edinburgh, and here again he and his acolytes were at the same glorious task.

John Bute was a man of unique inwardness. One wonders how few people there might be who really knew him well. But what he did for his contemporaries was splendid. A good citizen – a noble man who served his generation well – a terrible loss.

Raymond Edwards

I recall that when the Welsh College of Music and Drama was in Cardiff Castle, from its inception in 1949 until 1973 when it moved

On *King Duck* – the bibliophile, 1975.

Summer 1976 on *King Duck*, teasing Kopello.

Spring, 1978, Orkney. A rest or a bath?

Summer, 1978. A picnic on Bute, quite unaware that some ladies were stealthily approaching.

Skiing in Courcheval plus Andrew and Diana Percy, 1978.

12 November 1978. Wedding to Jennifer at Dumfries House.

26 April 1979, Johnny Dumfries's 21st. Lunch at the Glenburn Hotel. Misbehaving between Mrs MacDougall (housekeeper) and Miss Armit (archivist to three generations of Butes).

Christmas, 1979. Ndondela, White River, South Africa. Left to right, Andrew, Richard and Katherine Percy; John and Betty Home-Rigg; Diana Percy, plus dogs Thompson and Jane.

Autumn 1980. In America with
sister Fiona and brother-in-law
Michael Lowsley-Williams.

Christmas 1980. In small
drawing room at Mount Stuart.

Summer 1981. Bute Fabrics: Peter Simpson, Pat Grant and Harry Wagemanns.

Mount Stuart, April 1982.

Blue and Gold Ball, June 1983
– Anthony and Sophia
Crichton-Stuart.

Spring, 1984. With Jennifer and Muli Tang, the artist who painted John's portrait – the only one – in front of the Rock Garden at Mount Stuart.

16 October 1984. Dinner given for Raymond Edwards, Cardiff Castle: in front of portraits of the 3rd and 4th Marquesses.

November 1984. Shoot weekend staying with Archibald and Fiona Walker. John with Kopello with her leg in plaster in a plastic bag.

into the new building in College Park, Lord Bute would attend the meetings of the Castle Management Committee regularly. I attended from 1959 when I became Principal of the College.

I used to meet him during these visits, and I remember one meeting in particular. A City Councillor asked him if he would agree to the lowering of the Castle wall, opposite the Angel and the Crest Hotels in the main street. This would enable pedestrians to look over the wall and make them realise that there was a park there. Lord Bute retorted drily (he was a man of few words) that the wall existed at that height to prevent such a thing ever happening and that its purpose was to protect those who had chosen to go into it for solace and quiet, a haven free from the molestations of on-lookers and spectators. I thought that there was a little parable here – Are you on the outside looking in or on the inside looking out? The philistine Councillor was obviously on the outside looking in and could not appreciate that Bute Park had been secured for those people who had chosen to go there for peace and solitude, undisturbed by peeping Toms.

Needless to say the matter was not raised again. Bute Park, thanks to Lord Bute, has remained a lung for all the people of Cardiff and visitors to the city are filled with admiration for their sylvan centre. I am certain that the City Council would have forced a road or some such vandalism had not Lord Bute been vigilant at all times and insisted on safeguarding it for the populace.

Castle Management meetings were held in the small attractive room off the entrance hall, to the left of the Library. The entrance hall was the finishing point of the Castle tours. The guides would talk about the oak table which adorns the space and the stained glass windows – much admired by John Betjeman. One particular guide would make his peroration which included a potted version of the generosity of the Bute family to Cardiff. I was standing at the Library door and Lord Bute was standing just at the entrance to the Castle. We exchanged glances. I don't know to this day whether he approved of the guide's account, but the guide and his flock were unaware that the very same Lord was in their midst.

He was a great benefactor. The Welsh College of Music and Drama owes its existence to him. He gave permission for it to be housed in the Castle. It grew up there and when it had developed into a sturdy youth, he blessed it by making possible a site for the new

building on the edge of Bute Park. *Si vis monumentum, circumspice.*
We miss him.

Tom Errington

My first painting project at Mount Stuart was the ceiling in Jennifer's study, formerly the Smoking Room. When this was completed John wrote to me: 'Clearly any fears which you may have entertained of being haunted by the wrathful Billy Burges may be dismissed.' He further hoped I would become involved in other work in the house. Nearly six years later I am still there.

While I worked in the Horoscope Room we started to discuss the decoration of the Marble Chapel. Of all things John understood the importance of time to research and prepare. One evening during dinner he asked if I would find it useful to visit Zaragoza. Since the lantern in the Chapel is based on the design of the great cimborio in the Cathedral of La Seo in Zaragoza, I thought it would be a thrilling idea. 'Good,' said John, 'we have kept you from your family for long periods; I think you all should go.'

The original plan had been to paint eight saints in the alcoves round the drum of the lantern. But following the Zaragoza visit and encouraged by John to go to many other places and buildings, the concept expanded to include the upper cupola, the entire vault as well as the drum with its saints.

Most evenings for over two years when my visits to Mount Stuart corresponded with the Butes being at home, we would talk about the Chapel, painting, architecture and religion.

John hoped that in future the Marble Chapel could be used for the celebration of the Latin Tridentine Mass. He wistfully remarked on more than one occasion that since Vatican II High Anglicans have more fun than Roman Catholics.

When my visits did not coincide with the Butes I would find regular postcards waiting for me on my arrival. 'Do you realise there are nine ranks of Angel? I trust you are portraying the correct order!' Queen Margaret was to be included among the eight saints since John thought she was the first true European. We agreed she should have the twelve stars of Europe round the inside of her halo.

By the time I was ready to put a design on paper we had

[66]

discussed everything fully and I believe we both understood the other's thinking so clearly that no correction or changes were made. The most important thing was to make sure the final result was as perfect as it could be and we agreed that as the work proceeded changes should not be resisted if they were necessary at John's or my suggestion.

The scaffold was completed and by the spring of 1992 I was ready to start painting. I told John of my apprehension of working on such an enormous project, envisaged to take about thirty-five months. John laughed and told me that all who had seen my designs had approved and 'anyway there cannot be many people offering commissions of this size and nature today'.

John was a perfect patron and he enjoyed holding this position as much as everyone enjoyed working for him, becoming totally involved and caught up in his enthusiasm for Mount Stuart.

Just before he died, John and I were reviewing the progress in the Chapel. We came to discuss the eight saints which we had selected over a year ago. 'But we don't have St Magnus? St Magnus is my favourite saint.' We never did decide exactly where St Magnus should go. But he will be there.

Several years ago I had to take a taxi into Rothesay. During the journey my driver, a native of Bute, spoke of in-comers and their attitudes: 'When someone comes to the island and says it's all right for Lord Bute up in his castle, I say to them, if you go to Mount Stuart at eight in the morning you will find Lord Bute working at his desk, and if you go there at eight in the evening you will still find Lord Bute at his desk. And he doesn't get paid.'

Nicholas Fairbairn

I don't remember when I met him, but there was an instant electric click – because John was electric – electric in a thousand ways, although he nauseatingly (his favourite word) pretended not to be.

He was bestowed with everything – charm, wit, souciance, style, taste, sensitivity – and of least importance to him, riches, though they were the birdseed upon which his brilliance could thrive with irrelevant disregard for the consequences.

He spoilt me by asking me to Mount Stuart in his lonely years, until Jennifer's exotic energy gave back to him his indulgent unusuality. We had many wondersome times together, when I was hopefully helpful to a mighty mind, alone and astray, but never deserting his duty or his devotion to the majesty of Scotland's heritage and a myriad of other causes.

His company was unremitting fun and one of the most charming characteristics of his character was his disdain of conformity. I was made to shoot, but he didn't. I, as an Episcopalian, was made to go to Mass in the grand chapel, but he didn't attend. His brilliance was unique in its enormity. And what was so splendid about it was its nonchalance. For some squint reason, the term 'Your Grace' is reserved for clerics, for whom Johnnie had a most intelligent and graceful contempt. He was truly graceful. He never did anything ungraceful. He was the muse of Grace himself – in manners, in mood, in mode and in method. He graced every person he knew or met; and every undertaking he undertook. When the undertaker ungraciously took him away from us all, I'm sure he said some gracious words to him. He would, wouldn't he?

Anna Fekete

I only ever saw John twice in my life and even then the words we exchanged were fairly sparing. Also, I never knew him as most of the people who did spend time with him describe him. To me he never showed himself as somebody full of fun and unclouded merriness to the very core. I saw him laugh, I laughed at some of his jokes, but I was never sent any of his funny cards; and although I did love his sense of humour I always sensed something else beyond or underneath that. I never had the chance to confirm whether what my sixth sense was telling me about him was right or wrong. However, those impressions were very strong and they are the only foundation I can rely on when asked to talk about him.

Having said all that, he made an incredible difference to my life, partly through his generosity but perhaps even more by way of some subtle communication between us which – I hope it doesn't sound too arrogant – meant a lot to both of us. We hardly ever talked properly to each other and even through the mail we never overwhelmed each other with words. Yet there existed a very subtle, but strong tie between us which I never really understood or felt deserving of. Our relationship was always such that he was on the helping and giving end, I on the receiving; but I think my being – without any conscious act on my part or, again, without 'deserving' it – touched or stirred something in him. He must have known immense suffering to understand it so well in somebody else. How he came by this 'knowledge' I don't know. The only thing I can tell you with a fair amount of certainty about him is that he didn't know suffering and hardship – and by this I don't mean only physical, circumstantial hardship, but also mental suffering, the 'night of the soul' – from the outside, from looking at it and being sad and compassionate about it, from being moved by it, from wanting to help it. He knew it first hand; and therefore his way of relating to it and trying to help it had this quality or subtlety or 'feel' to it which simply defies description.

Martin Gardner

In first making contact with John in 1987, about possible sponsor-ship of a plant-collecting expedition to Chile, I had obviously struck lucky because of John's (and Jennifer's) keen interest in Chilean plants and their desire to diversify the planting in their much-cherished Wee Garden. In 1989 Sabina and I had our first oppor-tunity to visit Mount Stuart to discuss the results of our expedition and to inspect the plants that we had collected.

I had imagined Mount Stuart to be a smallish Scottish-type castle at the top of a rocky bluff. Of course I couldn't have been more wrong and we arrived at the front door with a certain feeling of trepidation. John was very welcoming and we had a most memorable stay. This was to be the first of many visits to the Isle of Bute. Most were in connection with Mount Stuart's involvement with the Conifer Conservation Programme. John's sense of humour was never very far away, especially the day when Dr Chris Page of the Conifer Programme turned up in a complete set of wet weather clothes and proceeded to change into something that he thought was more appropriate for lunch. As he removed his gumboots and pulled his slippers out of his briefcase in a most rehearsed manner, John remarked in a soft voice, 'Chris, I suppose you have your bathroom robe in there as well?'

John had a long and distinguished association with the Royal Botanic Garden, Edinburgh. Much of his energy was dedicated in serving on the board of the Younger (Benmore) Trust which included one of RBG Edinburgh's specialist gardens. For over twenty-six years John served on the board of Trustees, for sixteen of them as Chairman. In many ways the Conifer Conservation Programme started in 1989 when John floated the idea of using the Pinetum at Mount Stuart as an overflow for conifers from the Younger Botanic Garden. This was the first of a countrywide network of safe sites for the threatened conifers and Mount Stuart has continued to be one of the main sites for this important work.

I think it is very fitting that the Chilean rain forest project currently under construction at the Younger Botanic Garden, Benmore, is to be dedicated to John in recognition of his valuable work for RBG Edinburgh. It is also very appropriate because of his own family's close links with Chile and his desire to help others who were seeking stronger ties with that part of the world. Much of the collaborative conservation work that Edinburgh is currently involved with in Chile is largely due to John's unstinting efforts.

Stephen and Lavinia Gibbs

There was hardly a summer which went by without the arrival of *King Duck* on Arran to pick us up and take us on to a picnic spot. On board there would be a diverse assortment of interesting people, with John, who loved *King Duck*, at his most relaxed. Large Edwardian monogrammed hay boxes always contained an abundance of food and drink, laughter rang out continuously. Light-hearted teasing was one of John's favourite pastimes aboard and Jennifer ('Mrs Thatcher') came in for much of this. Friends' clothes were scrutinised and anything considered untoward or unsuitable was verbally torn apart – though only with those he knew could cope with such treatment. But the serious side of John also came out. He used *King Duck* to discuss and develop many of his new projects and interests; he always liked to know what others were doing, more so if he felt that it was a contribution to Scotland – for his desire to encourage Scotland's interests was paramount.

On longer trips to the Western Isles no effort was spared to see everything and anything of interest. Standing stones, brochs, castles and gardens were visited, be it by walking, on hired bicycles or in old cars miraculously hired by the Captain from some local inhabitant. Birds too were scrutinised and reference books keenly read; perhaps only wild flowers got off lightly. On Raasay John led us jubilantly through the window of the then near-derelict Raasay House to explore. In Lochboisdale harbour the tide went out leaving us high and dry on a rock. John spent the entire night off-loading all the heavy equipment, but mercifully the sea remained flat calm, the wind was still and at dawn we floated off unharmed – an unthinkable crisis averted.

King Duck gave enormous pleasure not only to John and Jennifer but to many others too. Happy memories of boating off the West Coast of Scotland will remain with them for many a day.

Jay L. Glaser

John and Jennifer Bute attended our Health Center for treatments designed to bring about rejuvenation, increased mind-body co-ordination and evoke a healing response based on the mind-body connection. At the time Jennifer's whole focus was on getting John to gain weight, since he was having a difficult time chewing and swallowing. John, however, was completely focused on gaining new knowledge and expanding his horizons. Even though he was somewhat weak, he plunged himself enthusiastically into learning Transcendental Meditation, practising yoga, learning yogic breathing exercises, and learning the ancient Ayurvedic theories on health and healing. In spite of his weakened condition he revelled in long walks in the woods. When at the end of the week he still had not gained any weight, I pointed out that he should spend more time eating. He laughed heartily and then promptly engaged me in a lively intellectual discussion of Ayurvedic theory and meditation. Our whole staff was impressed by his keen wit, intellect and concern for others, even though he was the one that needed the most attention.

[71]

Bobby Gordon

During a shooting weekend in Suffolk, some thirty-three years ago, I remember going on the train back to London and Lord Bute saying 'Well, I hope you've got plenty of money, because I haven't a penny; I gave it all away on tips.'

Always at Mount Stuart shoots – when there were normally eight guns – Lord Bute would take the worst beat himself.

Once, when driving to Milngavie for a duck shoot, Lord Bute stopped to ask directions and was told by the person asked: 'You go straight up there, Jock, and along. . .' Lord Bute smiled and politely thanked him.

John Greenall

I first met John when I was six and he was a lot older! At the time our preparatory school, West Downs, was housed at Blair Castle, in order to avoid Herr Hitler's V1s and V2s and provide accommodation for the military. Every cat burglar in Britain had attempted to open His Grace of Atholl's safe to no avail. John achieved this feat with a 'tanner' or old sixpenny piece. His rear end bore ample evidence of the headmaster's view of his achievement.

Despite his early exploits, or maybe because he learned somewhat painfully from them, John was one of the kindest and most selfless men I have ever met, although he possessed a wicked sense of humour. I well recall him decanting the contents of Jennifer's suitcase out of the bedroom window at home when they came to stay for the weekend. On another occasion he sent me a card apparently covered in Chinese. When turned upside down it read 'Bugger you and Santa too!'

When we went to stay at Mount Stuart he taught my children quite appalling habits such as flicking butter pats up to the ceiling with table napkins; he openly called their mother 'Jimmy', and Jennifer 'Mrs Thatcher'. He liked nothing more than to be given a practical joke as a present. You sat down in an armchair at your peril because, more often than not, the Whoopsey cushion that you gave him last time would blast out at you.

He used to send my younger daughter dreadful postcards from all parts of the globe – so dreadful that they normally required envelopes! With her there was a marvellous bond, which manifested itself only too clearly in her devastation when he died.

I last saw him about six weeks before his death. I was having lunch in Edinburgh with a friend and I introduced him to John. In his own inimitable fashion John told him he should stitch up his trouser pockets whilst in my company – who needs enemies with friends like that?

Very quietly and unobtrusively he did a great deal for Scotland. He was very special and is greatly missed.

Donald Hardie

Elegance marked every aspect of John – elegance of manner, of movement, of thought – whether in the chair at a meeting or in the shooting field. In the chair at a company board meeting, the elegance of his manner led everyone else to the same quiet approach – but always conscious that he had done his homework, knew his facts, had considered the problem and, in his own mind, had found an answer or a new strategy, even though he always waited quietly and patiently to hear the views and suggestions of others. Then, as the decision was taken, he would put on his serious look and tell the board about the different people he had already approached to seek help or advice or action. And all the time everyone knew that his remarkable memory could recall comments or details put forward at previous meetings. I used to ask him about his vast range of knowledge – 'Ah,' he would say, 'but I read when I travel around Scotland, and in hotels where I have to stay.'

Spending a night at Mount Stuart used to be an endurance test. The evenings passed with one fascinating subject after another, accompanied by repeated 'little dribbles' of whisky. Then, late into the night, John suddenly dropped the serious talk and became mischievous and entertaining. His sense of fun, most obvious late at night, was always liable to surface – often at his own expense, never malicious or wounding or cynical.

[73]

Always there was the strong commitment to the community, to Scotland's present based on the past. This showed itself in many ways but for me an intriguing example was the concept of creating a permanent corps on to which could be grafted volunteers in the vacation and holiday periods. He sent me off to see if I could interest organisations in seconding staff for, say, six months a year. Cadets from the Police, Fire and Ambulance service, Army personnel – all agreed to participate, although the Army was reluctant. It was hoped construction companies would lend equipment and staff to help projects like clearing city dereliction, footpaths, canals, bridges, recreation areas. The scheme withered because it proved too complicated to set up a management team to co-ordinate all the projects, staff and finance. Pity – it would have been a remarkable memorial to a man of rare vision.

His love of Mount Stuart and all its details was obvious in so many ways. In his last three months he wanted to show me the progress towards the completion of the decoration of the Marble Chapel; so he took me up the ladders, up past the scaffolding floor. As we looked at yet another ladder, I said 'John, are you sure you should be doing this?' At the quiet answer, 'No', we started down - but he had shared his plans and hopes with me and let me see his vision for the continuation of a family project.

Being in John's presence was always special, with expectations of fun, of new ideas and knowledge, of thoughts set in the framework of his interests, of challenges and projects. There was a deep undercurrent that held people to him, so that always I felt sorry when it came time to part and always I felt I would do anything he asked of me – and I did.

Sally Hardie

John Bute had so many qualities which he generously gave to his friends and his country and which were an example to others. His quiet, elegant manner belied his intellect and his strong purposeful leadership, his vision and his energy, and also his enjoyment of wit and fun in the fullest sense. When relaxed, in the mood, and in the right company to set him off, he was the greatest of fun – clowning with the best – or worst – of them. He was, too, a true friend –

one when needed and unasked. I never heard him speaking ill of anyone. He preferred to keep those thoughts to himself. He did, however, often take the role of the devil's advocate.

The National Trust for Scotland provided for him a vehicle worthy of his talents, enabling him to develop and exercise them in the service of a high and lasting purpose. Both John and the Trust benefited greatly from this association.

As a leader he was remarkable. His knowledge was encyclopaedic, as was his memory, his handling of people friendly and skilled. He didn't boss, he led, he knew where he was going and we all followed. I think this quality, coupled with his modesty, brought out the best in people and set a pattern of selfless service to a visionary cause.

He often spoke of the pursuit of excellence. He was, in the breadth of his interest and knowledge, a modern Renaissance man, an innovative patron of the arts and crafts, encouraging and supporting the skills and talents of the new and the young, while still appreciating and conserving the best of the old.

One could write a book about this exceptional man – who lit up the lives of those he knew and served.

Marshall J. Harris

I first met Lord Bute in the spring of 1959, soon after I had become Scottish National Officer of the United Nations Association (UNA). John had become a Vice President of UNA in 1956, having accepted the position because he wanted to be identified with the refugee problem and to show some leadership in Scotland where a national appeal was being mounted to help refugees in Europe.

Our first meeting was a faltering series of unrelated chat because we were both shy and the others present were no better. When I returned to my office I wrote to him and apologised for not raising the issues that should have been the purpose of our meeting. Within three days I received an invitation to Mount Stuart and from then on we had a most warm and sincere friendship.

He was a great Scot with an enormous capacity to remember people and detail. Our common interest was international affairs, particularly the United Nations. He rationed his interests in order that he could give time, money and thought on how best to promote the cause.

During my twenty-eight years working for UNA he was most supportive and was very influential in creating the Bute Branch of the Association. Whenever possible he was willing to be involved in the many activities.

In 1986 The Scottish Educational Trust for UN and International Affairs was set up and he accepted the office of Chairman. Not only did he become Chairman, he was also benefactor and leader; someone who knew how to get the best results from limited resources. He disliked glossy publicity material, he felt it was a waste of money.

In spite of his status and opportunity to mix with the great and the good, at all times he was humble and not given to criticism of other people. His charming way of introducing someone was quite unique. It was never a problem to be in his company; he had the ability to make everyone feel at ease.

As our relationship grew and we began to understand each other better, he would chide me for not getting out sooner the minutes of meetings. He knew I had a dislike for writing minutes and reminded me by saying 'I think it is better to get the minutes out before the next meeting.'

I well remember my first visit to Mount Stuart in 1959. I was nervous when I arrived at Rothesay to be met by a chauffeur-driven car. John and I chatted about the UN and at 3 p.m. we went to the nursery and for an hour we were considerably abused by three extremely active children; hair was pulled and John and I were their targets for whatever they felt like doing. At 4 p.m. precisely the nannies returned and we withdrew. It took a little time to recover. He made me feel very much a member of the family at all times.

On another occasion when I was over at Bute, nineteen people sat down for lunch and I was the only person without a title. That made no difference to John; rank did not matter.

We once motored to Carlisle to the headquarters of Border TV. The young lady asked John who he was. 'John Bute,' he said. She promptly introduced him to the managing director by saying 'Mr Bute is here to see you.' John only laughed.

In his leadership of the Scottish Educational Trust for United Nations and International Affairs he took a close interest in its projects and attended all the Trust meetings until illness made it impossible to continue. On one occasion I suggested that he become President and thereby reduce the number of meetings he had to attend. His reply was that his time was not important.

A further quality which made him different from most people of this age is that he never failed to write and say thank you for even a small act of kindness, taking him out for a meal, sending him something to mark an occasion. He was a perfect gentleman.

So many instances of note pass through my mind when I survey a long and sincere relationship with John that it is difficult to itemise all the details. I would rather summarise the qualities of the relationship which have left heartfelt memories for me to treasure for the rest of my life:

He was a shy man but he kept his relationships in constant repair.

He put much effort into his interests to ensure their success.

He put others before self on almost all occasions.

He was determined in his work to achieve the highest possible quality, whatever the project. He did not appreciate second best.

These are my memories of John Crichton-Stuart.

Clare Henry

The Marquess of Bute's death robbed Scotland if its foremost ambassador for its arts and crafts. A man of great integrity, charm and kindness, he worked tirelessly as chairman, president and trustee of innumerable committees and boards including the Royal Museums of Scotland, National Trust for Scotland and Scottish National Portrait Gallery. Never flamboyant, always sincere, he was that rare thing: an old-fashioned aristocrat who believed that privilege brought with it a duty to be of service to both nation and community.

One venture close to Lord Bute's heart was Edinburgh Dovecot Tapestry Company founded by his grandfather in 1912; a unique creative force for over eighty years. There are few places in the world nowadays that still retain the weaving skills necessary for important, large-scale tapestries and the Dovecot is famous for its interpretations of works by top-rank contemporary artists such as

[77]

David Hockney, Graham Sutherland, Frank Stella, Sir Eduardo Paolozzi, Elizabeth Blackadder, Sir Robin Philipson and Adrian Wiszniewski. Following John Bute's death it was at risk. The recession and lack of orders left the Dovecot in bad shape financially, despite its worldwide reputation, and morale was severely dented by the loss of John Bute who was its central pillar. However, a memorial to Lord Bute in the form of a tapestry woven there could and should make all the difference.

One of John's last concerns was to try to secure the Dovecot by ensuring continuing commissions which would keep this unique workshop going for years to come. Only days before his death a major commission (creating work for two years) for a large £160,000 tapestry for London's new £500m British Library was turned down at a late stage due to Government cuts. This seemed the final straw. Ironically the project had been instigated by the Government and announced by the then Arts Minister, Richard Luce, in 1989.

John's dearest wish was to see the continuation of the commissioning of new art and new crafts. To this end he ensured that projects begun by artists for his own family home, Mount Stuart at Rothesay, would continue. Even his funeral took place against the setting of a new tapestry based on the Book of Revelations, commissioned by him from James More.

The vast seven-metre-square British Library tapestry (inspired by Kitaj's painting *If Not, Not* in the Scottish National Gallery) had already been started when John Bute died. So why not make this tapestry, destined for the twentieth century's most ambitious new building, as a memorial to Lord Bute? That it would be woven at the Dovecot Tapestry Company which owes its existence to the Butes, providing work for all their weavers for a long period, would be particularly fitting.

In 1993 the idea was given welcome backing by the Bute family, together with many key people, who saw it as a splendid and highly appropriate idea. Minister Lord James Douglas-Hamilton spoke as MP for Edinburgh West which includes the Dovecot: 'I find the workshop enormously impressive. The Bute memorial would be a splendid plan.' Sir Nicholas Fairbairn went further: 'It would be ironic and tragic if one of the inspired concepts of John Bute was to die with him. Its future and salvation should spring from the earth in which he is buried as a tribute to him. Let us ensure that this Dovecot tapestry, merely one of the many artistic children he patronised, comes to realisation and glory.'

The British Library, due to open in 1996, had been dogged by ill fortune, not least a cut in its funding due to Government implementation of 17½% VAT – which incidentally adds £28,000 to the cost of the tapestry. This provoked a scandal in 1991 when Government's decision to renege on its commitment to commissioned works of art, several like the Dovecot tapestry already begun, created headlines as the Library's independent art committee resigned *en bloc*. Lord Bute was uncharacteristically outspoken: 'I regard it as a betrayal. We had an agreement. It's also an act of the gravest philistinism,' he told me at the time.

The vast soaring Library atrium is now complete and looks impressive, bar the towering left-hand brick wall of the entrance hall made especially to take, and crying out for, the missing Dovecot tapestry. Its architect, Colin St John Wilson, emphasises, 'The tapestry is not an extra. It is an integral, underlying part of the building. Would you call the stained glass in Chartres Cathedral an extra? It is part and parcel of the building. When the Queen eventually opens the Library a blank wall will look pretty shameful.' Brian Lang, Chief Executive of the British Library, is equally keen that the Kitaj Dovecot tapestry be realised, once the money can be found.

John Bute was one of the most civilised and creative men I have known. No doubt there will be many tributes to him – but what better memorial than something which he himself had worked so hard to achieve and which, significantly, would be made by his own Dovecot weavers in Scotland yet seen in London's premier twentieth-century public building, visited by well over a million people each year.

Since John's death his daughter, Sophie, has taken his place as Dovecot Chairman, working hard to secure commissions – including a splendid tapestry, funded by Alastair Salvesen, for Edinburgh's new 1994 Festival Theatre and Kate Whiteford's tapestry for the new wing of the Royal Scottish Museum. The Dovecot having turned the corner, she intends to keep it that way – but the British Library tapestry would, she underlines, secure things admirably.

When Lord Bute died Johnny Noble put it well: 'John was

[79]

completely selfless and unsparing in his commitment to Scotland and to the arts. It was a great disappointment to him that the Library tapestry did not come to fruition. A memorial tapestry is a wonderful idea; a chance to set the balance right and make his dream come true. I very much hope it happens.' I'm sure Sophie agrees with Johnny Noble's sentiments. I know I do.

Antony Hornyold

John in his early teens looked very innocent but was ready to enter into any mischief going. He and David, coming from Bute, and my brother and I, coming from Sutherland, used to meet up with Andrew and Peregrine Bertie in Edinburgh for the journey back to Ampleforth by train to York.

We generally succeeded in getting a compartment to ourselves and, once established in one, few were tempted to join us. One prosperous-looking gentleman who did so became extremely irate on discovering that he had sat on a large bar of chocolate. I cannot remember who was responsible for putting it there, or indeed whether it got there by accident or design, but I have a strong recollection of John at the time, apparently engrossed in his book, and the last person anyone would suspect of misusing chocolate.

Jocelyn Humfrey

'A wish to produce exceptional things exceptionally well' was the principal aim behind the founding of Recollections by John Bute in 1984. The idea of basing a company on the manufacture of high-quality replicas was novel. He and his great friend Anna Plowden believed that there was enormous scope for a company which based itself upon the highest principles to reproduce replicas of a few of the vast array of beautiful items housed in Britain's museums, galleries and country houses. Additionally, the aim was to use only British craftsmen and to promote museum trading through the auspices of the company. These were fundamental to Recollections and were adhered to throughout the ten years the company existed. High-quality design and craftsmanship were integral to it.

To start a company of this kind with such ideals was typical of Lord Bute. His ability to combine modern designs and approaches with antique pieces was clear in his furnishing of 15 Queen Anne's Gate, which was where Recollections was based. He was a tireless supporter of the young craftsmen in this country and the founding of Recollections was just one of the many ways he put his support into practice.

The objects sold by Recollections came from a wide variety of places. The first collection of solid silver items, launched to coincide with the Treasure House exhibition in the United States, was an example of modern copies of fine pieces of silver with no expense spared in the manufacture and presentation. The results were magnificent. Many collections and objects were to follow from the Burrell Museum in Glasgow, the Victoria and Albert Museum, Woburn Abbey, a large number of National Trust houses, and so the list goes on. The objects ranged from Roman busts and medieval bronzes to fine bone china birds, English silver and glass. All sales of Recollections objects carried a royalty which was paid to further the work and aims of the originating source.

As the outgoing MD of Recollections it was with very great sadness that I watched the company disappear with the tragic and untimely death of Lord Bute. In my time at Recollections John Bute instilled in the small team that worked for it a remarkable solidarity and understanding of the aims. Loyalty was a basic theme and this was something you found whenever dealing with his marvellous staff at Mount Stuart and elsewhere.

I was allowed by Lord Bute to take my rather wild border terrier, Macduff, to work. He became the self-appointed guardian of the whole of Queen Anne's Gate, much to my embarrassment and the irritation, I suspect, of the rest of the office. However, Lord Bute's amazing tolerance of this invasion was soon made clear. On the first day Macduff decided that Lord Bute's office was clearly the place to be (something which was to continue throughout my stay at QAG). Unfortunately there was a meeting of some importance taking place that first morning. Macduff, having been found running round Lord Bute's chair, was gently removed to my desk with the query as to whether he was anything to do with me. This was a subject I was to be teased about by Lord Bute for the rest of my time at Recollections.

A great deal of very hard work went into the selection of the items made for and sold by Recollections. The team consisted of many highly talented and erudite people. These included Michael Trinick and Frank Potter with their wide and intricate knowledge of many national museums and the National Trust; Roy Wadland and George O'Brien with their excellent design talent and knowledge of the Potteries; Anna Plowden with her vast expertise as a conservator; and Serena Fass, to mention but a few. On one occasion the entire crew departed on a train with Lord Bute to visit Castell Coch, a property formerly owned by the Butes and now in the care of CADW – Welsh Historic Monuments. An early start was followed by a large English breakfast. It was not until the end of the journey that the prolonged absence of Anna Plowden was noticed. It was then discovered that Anna had spent a large part of the journey stuck in the 'ladies' (if such a thing can be said to exist on a British Rail train), whence her hammerings and shouts had gone unheeded by her fellow travellers. This was something often referred to at Board lunches, much to the embarrassment of the lady concerned.

My six years with Recollections were punctuated by Lord Bute's humour. Once when I had been instructed to bid for an item at Sotheby's on his behalf, I admitted to having 'got on the wrong foot' and bid more than I had been instructed. This could have been an expensive moment for me – John Bute mildly commented that the item had gone far higher than the estimate and on this occasion it was clearly lucky I had missed it! A mistake I did not make again on my forays into the major auction houses in London on his behalf.

My final and lasting memory of John Bute was some weeks before he died, when Recollections was much reduced in size and he himself clearly extremely unwell. He rang me to thank me for my work . . . An example to remember and follow.

Peter Jones

Stillness was the clue to so many of John's virtues: it underpinned and recharged his sensitivity and intelligence, his style and his service. The range of his courtesies, from absolute punctuality to doric postcards, remained either undetected or incomprehensible to many of their recipients. His silences sometimes, and judiciously, bewildered the bumptious, but the protective privacy of silences was more important to him than competitive badinage. Silence at breakfast, over the newspaper; silence in contemplating the qualities of space and light, of materials and workmanship – on visits by Museum Trustees he would invariably disappear by himself to savour the delights and detail of a building or artefact; silences in listening to others and in reflecting upon the complexities of an issue. And finally: laughter. That extraordinary explosion of sound, half cackle, by which he seemed often to surprise himself as much as others. Laughter, which broke the silence, the solitude, and their attendant, melancholy, and once more invited communion with others. Laughter which was already signalled, to the observant, in those iridescent cufflinks and effulgent neckties.

Over drinks or dinner we would speculate on how to achieve yet greater disasters than those we had embarrassingly seen elsewhere – leaking roofs, crumbling concrete, uncleanable windows, corroded metal, ghastly restaurants, unspeakable loos; could we manage all those in one glorious monstrosity? On two occasions we could not find the entrance to a prestigious new museum building. On another we were shown a magnificent consolidated power and security system. We were seated in the basement control room and the crucial switch was thrown: total darkness and paralysis ensued. 'Fred,' screamed a distraught official, 'have you got a screwdriver?' John declared, later, that since we already had a screwdriver we did not need the rest of the system. His interest in anything large-scale was grounded in impeccable miniaturism, since the result and the quality alike resided in the smallest detail. Poor workmanship distressed him intensely – it was, to him, a moral fault: his comments on the finish of the Pyramid extension to the Louvre, based on precise and minute inspection, were damningly succinct. And, of course, the reason is obvious. For John there could be no gap between a man and his works: 'le style, c'est l'homme même'.

Dick Kingzett

John and I organised two exhibitions at Agnew's in aid of the National Trust for Scotland. The staff of that splendid organisation, all of whom would have laid down their lives for him, were wonderful people to work with, but without John's – and of course Jennifer's – enthusiasm and diplomatic skill, I doubt that in either case we would have got the show on the road. The first, 'Dutch and Flemish Pictures from Scottish Collections', probably concentrated more major works of art from the Low Countries in our Top Gallery than have ever come together there during the 176 years of our firm's history. The second was of the pictures from Fyvie Castle which had recently been taken over by the Trust. It had been put together in the late 1890s by one of our more idiosyncratic clients, Sir Alexander Forbes-Leith, and its essentially Scottish character is demonstrated by the fact that it contained thirteen portraits by Sir Henry Raeburn. It was, as John predicted, the more popular of the two exhibitions.

I also helped him with the sale of two pictures – Cuyp's *Landscape with Horseman and Peasants* and Saenredan's *Interior of St Bavo, Haarlem*. He was rightly determined that both pictures should remain in this country, but as each was by common consent the greatest work painted by the artist, considerable amounts of money were involved. John's extraordinary ability to keep everyone with whom he dealt happy without ever losing their respect made my part in the proceedings a very congenial and rewarding one.

John saw things in a big way. When my wife and I bought a house in Gloucestershire, our arrival coincided with a murderous bout of Dutch elm disease. Our immediate priority was to plant a small shelter belt of some quick-growing species, in whose lee we could eventually develop more permanent things. I asked John for advice. He suggested *Nothofagus alessandri*, a Chilean beech, adding 'But I shouldn't put in more than a thousand at first.' I lacked the courage to tell him that I really only had about twenty in mind.

Although a man who achieved much in an intensely practical way, he had also an unworldly side. Staying with him at Dumfries House, I realised after a dinner party that he was starting a heavy cold. My own sovereign remedy on these occasions is a hot toddy and it was agreed that this was a good idea. Whisky and lemons were readily available on the drinks tray, but honey – the third vital ingredient – proved more difficult. Someone suggested a visit to the kitchen, but John looked vague and the project was abandoned.

Only later did I realise that he probably had little or no idea where the kitchen was.

After the first of the exhibitions I have mentioned above, to my great delight he made me a Life Member of the Trust, and my delight was enhanced when I discovered he had done the same for my secretary, our foreman and our van driver at Agnew's.

One obituary described him as an eighteenth-century figure born out of time. Well yes, but one might go back even further. The Duke Federigo da Montefeltro of Urbino, one of the foremost patrons of painters, sculptors and architects of the Renaissance, formed a wonderful library as well as being a consummate politician and a brilliant general. When his librarian asked him what was the most important qualification for a leader of men, Montefeltro replied, 'Essere umano' – that is, 'to be human'. The 6th Marquess of Bute and that Duke of Urbino had much in common.

Alison Kinnaird

On one of my visits to Mount Stuart to fit panels for the screen in John's office, I happened to have my children, Ellen and John, with me as they were on their half-term holiday. They were amazed by the house and all its treasures and fascinated by the way of applying gold leaf to the ceiling paintings that Tom Errington showed them.

When a tall gentleman greeted us kindly and directed us upstairs to see the secret passage, they asked me 'Who was that?' 'That was Lord Bute,' I answered. 'It can't be, he was wearing red corduroy trousers,' was the reaction. I'm not sure what they expected him to wear – perhaps a coronet and robes – but they definitely were not prepared for John's colourful style!

My own abiding impression of him is of his kindness and the quiet good taste with which he directed and encouraged the projects that I took part in at Mount Stuart. He allowed the artists to produce the very best work of which they were capable, while creating a work of art with which both patron and artist were completely satisfied. I feel very honoured to have some of my work as part of the interior of Mount Stuart, which will remain as such a lasting reminder of his interests, enthusiasms and love of the arts.

Fitzroy Maclean

It is not easy to capture John on paper. When he was young, my first impression was a tall, good-looking, well turned out ex-public schoolboy with a pleasant, urbane manner and not a lot between the ears. It was definitely misleading. I soon found I was on the wrong track, and whether this was because of his natural modesty, or equally natural desire to tease, I was never quite sure.

Second time round most people readjusted their bearings. Was it the understated but careful perfection of his clothes? The delight he took in consulting and learning from all the experts? The self-deprecating remark that often astonished one by its astuteness and knowledge? Or the quiet aside that often pricked the pomposity of others?

John loved perfection: it was always his ultimate goal – but it was not an aesthetically cold perfection – he was much too earthy for that – and the warmth and simplicity of his character showed in a hundred different ways.

The schoolboy bit was right – in a way. Like many diffident and very private people who find it difficult to communicate, John relied on the banter and affectionate ragging of adolescence to consolidate friendship. But there was something so intrinsically good and decent about the man that he made friends everywhere – and in every world – and kept them, for no one took more trouble with his friends than he did.

He bore the ever-increasing weight of public service lightly – as if it were a natural and perfectly acceptable corollary of the privilege he had been born to, but his sense of duty and of service came from the heart, and not from what was 'expected' of him. His workload towards the end of his life was enormous, but when he was 'off duty' no one was a better organiser of fun.

Two happy memories come uppermost to mind. The first was very Highland – a sea visit between sea neighbours that, clan history apart, might easily have occurred in the eighteenth century. The *Dodo* (later *King Duck*) had sailed up Loch Fyne from the Kyles and had anchored off Fitzroy's 'second best' pier, a small boat was lowered and in the golden light of a perfect summer evening we embarked, gumboots below full-dress finery, to sail across the loch to Minard, where our host, young Campbell of Succoth, equally splendid in velvet and tartan, was waiting for us, with a boat hook to hand. We walked a trifle unsteadily up to his house, for our party had already begun on board the *Dodo*, and how we walked down again I don't really remember, but I do know we had to wake the captain.

The second was a more exotic affair. *Dorita,* a yacht chartered by John, had sailed up the Adriatic with his Lordship and family aboard, to pay the island of Korcula, which lies off the Dalmatian coast, an official visit and, quite incidentally, to have fun with the Macleans. (The island of Bute had been 'twinned' with the island of Korcula in a moment of enthusiasm by its council and its MP.) All had gone well and everyone on Korcula had been delighted by Lord Bute, the children and the easy geniality and hospitality of a Scottish lord. We visited and were entertained in every village of the island and it was almost an afterthought that the Korculans decided we must pay the Mayor of Orebic, a mainland village across the Kanal, a visit too or their feelings would be hurt.

Here I must digress, as this visit was not quite so simple as we believed it to be. For, after the war had ended, the Korculan partisans, in a moment of over-excitement, had strung up the Mayor's father for being a German collaborator. When they found out later he hadn't been one after all, they apologised and, to make amends, asked his son to be Mayor – for life.

This was the gentleman we were to visit and when John asked me how he should be dressed, I answered 'Oh, bum bags and sandshoes and perhaps a T-shirt, they're very informal in Orebic.'

But, alas, as we approached the Orebic pier, it became evident that I was wrong and informality was not the order of *that* day, for a magnificent figure in a *circa* 1900 black frock coat and top hat advanced towards the gang plank, surrounded by a troupe of young ladies in national costume, bearing bouquets, and another of young men in nautical rig who let off fire crackers and blew trumpets. Poor John descended the ladder, trying to look as dignified as possible, but hopping about a bit as the *feu de joie* exploded round his feet, risking grave damage, as he later pointed out, to his undercarriage. It needed all his charm and experience to retrieve the situation, but retrieve it he did, and though he swore he would never forgive me, that visit too turned out to be a great success.

[87]

Mark Marlesford

I was lucky enough to stay at Mount Stuart quite often in the 1950s and 60s. It was rather like being in a Renaissance Florentine court – surrounded by treasures, feasting on delicacies such as chanterelle from the beech woods on which the Italian or French chef had worked wonders, and presided over by an enchanting and wholly benign princely host in John.

John McVey

A number of years ago, Lord Bute's then Head Gardener – John McVey, my uncle – was a very dour, crusty and extremely staid character. He had served three Marquesses and could certainly be said to be an estate institution. At that time Mass was celebrated every Sunday at Mount Stuart and the Head Gardener would be there, sitting in the same seat as he always sat in. This particular Sunday, one of Lord Bute's guests, unaware of the seating arrangements, sat in the Head Gardener's place.

After Mass his Lordship took the guest aside as said, 'George, you did something I would be afraid to do – you sat in old McVey's seat. Life on the estate, I'm afraid, will never be the same for any of us again!'

In 1958 a number of Bute shotgun enthusiasts wanted to re-establish the defunct Bute Gun Club. They approached the then Bute Estate factor, Mr Milligan, with a request for a site to set up two clay pigeon traps. Mr Milligan duly mentioned it to Lord Bute and asked what he thought of the proposal. After pondering for a few moments his Lordship said, 'I think it would be a good idea. If they are blasting away at clay pigeons, maybe they will leave my pheasants alone.'

Hanne Mason

A very vivid memory is of the day of my first interview at 15 Queen Anne's Gate, London, when Lord Bute himself opened the door and showed me into, I thought, a very old-fashioned office (where in later years I was to enjoy working in a very comfortable, modern, refurbished flat). He had obviously made notes of what questions to ask and did so for a little while, before suggesting that perhaps a drink would be a good idea. A very relaxed interview, to which I had looked forward with trepidation!

Lord Bute's very many public roles and multitude of involvements and interests meant that my work was never dull or boring, although the ever-increasing filing system gave many a headache.

Such was the respect in our office for Lord Bute's letter-writing and very rich vocabulary that on one occasion in my early days I remember my audio-typing colleague agonising for hours over a word which sounded like 'your "pissy" letter'. Eventually she had to give in and obtain the correct one of 'pithy' from Lord Bute, who chuckled as only he could.

I marvelled at the way he – apparently so easily – pulled together all aspects of a particular matter requiring solution and in very few words resolved what many people and several committee meetings had failed to do. He always took his time arriving at a decision and obtained all expert advice necessary before making up his mind – and did not easily change it again thereafter.

Lord Bute was in every way one of the very few real gentlemen who understood the human being astonishingly well. I was constantly surprised by the courteous way he treated everyone with whom he had dealings and by the rare gift he had of giving you his full attention, to make you understand he was really interested – and he *always* made time. He constantly thought of others, even in the later stages of his illness when he was worried (and even apologising) that he was unable to do some of the tasks that needed his direction.

This is not to say he was at all above gentle mockery. I remember the first and only time I gave him a lift to the ferry (because the then butler was drunk) in my new car, which I immediately stalled. My distinguished passenger commented 'I'm impressed.'

Even during his illness there were many jolly moments because of his way of carrying on: when he 'played hookie' and came to his office in defiance of strict instructions from doctor, wife and nurse, there were many chuckles and jibes about the liquid foods he had tried to relish.

[89]

Such was the excellence with which Lord Bute carried out every task and duty, and imbued in his staff, that on the day I might have to leave my employment at Mount Stuart, I determined to put a notice on my office door saying 'Still in pursuit of excellence'!

James J. More

I first met John when he interviewed me for the position of Managing Director of one of his companies, the Edinburgh Tapestry Company Ltd. I had already had an exhaustive day's discussions with the Deputy Chairman and one of the company's directors when I arrived at an exclusive Edinburgh hotel for an interview with the company's Chairman, the Marquess of Bute. I had never met a marquess before and was extremely nervous.

The Deputy Chairman met me in the foyer and settled me into a large leather armchair while he went off to inform Lord Bute I had arrived. Anxiety was beginning to test my resolve, when an elegant but casually dressed gentleman stopped by my table on his way from an inner lounge to the front door. As he delved into the dish of peanuts sitting on my table, he asked if the rain had stopped. Our conversation moved from the weather to the impending refurbishment of the hotel and its remarkable hospitality in providing peanuts so early on in the day. I mentioned peanuts always seemed to taste so much better when thrown up and caught midair. With nonchalant ease my companion began tossing nuts into the air. I followed suit, but thoughts of my impending interview cramped my style. As the third nut bounced off my nose to skitter away across the carpet, I caught sight of the Deputy Chairman coming round the corner. Guilt merged with panic. I shot to my feet knocking the table sideways, throwing the dish of peanuts to the floor. Relief flooded over me as I realised he was alone. 'Ah,' he said, 'there you are. I've been looking all over for you, Lord Bute. I'm so glad to see you've found Mr More.' As I looked at my companion he popped his last remaining peanut into his mouth.

I worked with John for six very wonderful years. For me they were a voyage of personal discovery and delight. John was an exacting boss who expected much from his staff. But his kind and generous spirit, his unambiguous enthusiasm and loyal support, and his unparalleled wisdom made it easy to excel. Indeed, excellence was a byword for staff in his companies. Each shared their Chairman's ambition to give a lead to a cultural, commercial renaissance through quality achieved by skill, integrity, courageous innovation and design, and sensible product marketing. John was a very private man, but I never found him to be more than a phone call away, a very special friend who always understood and seemed always effortlessly to encourage.

At least once a year he and Jennifer would disappear to some very lost part of the world. On one such trip he sent me a postcard from the darkest jungle in Malaysia suggesting it was time to produce a new brochure for the company. It had to be 'first class', of course. On his return I enquired how he came to post my card from such an inhospitable place. 'Oh,' he said, 'I came across a post box in a clearing.' It made me wonder if he ever passed a post box without using it for some of his legendary cards. He told me he had a postcard for every occasion, and I could well believe it. They would tease, admonish, praise, instruct, inform, chat and invite, each one dated and beautifully written in black ink, the image part of the sense for the receiver. As in his small, cream, one-side-only letters, his mastery of language was superb, his sense of humour, fun and cheek never far away. I was once chided for writing to him about a 'choir' of angels, provoking a quick response of an Andy Warhol card of cherubs telling me unequivocally, 'It is a *host* of angels.' In another card showing Dunnotter Castle perched high on its rock surrounded by a cold, unfriendly sea, John commented that it must have been a 'hell of a sweat delivering the morning milk and newspapers'.

We would often dine together. Sometimes it was a quiet supper, at other times a reception meal. I was forever losing my napkin, and would often meet John under the table retrieving his own. John was the perfect host and normally the most engaging guest. However, there were times when his teasing got out of hand and provoked unexpected results. Once, at a dinner in Glasgow, an exasperated lady member of one of his committees threw a very large, very pink napkin at him with greater accuracy than the lob deserved. It fell on his head covering his face completely. He made no move to remove it but continued to converse. 'I suspect you will think this my better side,' he said. 'Only slightly,' his bantering partner replied, as she continued airing her views to his pink veil.

The last time I saw John was only a few days before he died. He was much slighter in his figure than he had been, and more frail, but, as ever, he was impeccably dressed. His eyes sparkled with the same intelligence and his presence imbued the same familiar confidence and strength. Though speech was difficult and painful for him, he spoke with great determination to be understood, and to disguise his discomfort. His counsel held no less weight and his sense of fun was no less diminished. We spoke of many things before discussing his plans for the future of his much loved Dovecot Studios of the Edinburgh Tapestry Company. When it came time for me to leave he rested his right hand on my shoulder, as he so often did. Only in his final words as he wished me goodbye and good luck was familiarity dispelled. Was he even then so many steps ahead of me, knowing we would not meet again?

John Mott

John was passionate from the start that Culzean Country Park, Scotland's first under the Countryside (Scotland) Act 1967, should be a resounding success. This was an experiment in cooperation under which the National Trust for Scotland, which owned the land inalienably, would continue to develop and operate the Park to a policy agreed by a joint committee of the local authorities of Ayr County, the Burghs of Ayr and Kilmarnock. It is to John's lasting credit that due to his leadership and persuasive charm these authorities, by no means the happiest of bedfellows on other matters, combined so cheerfully and effectively. Bill Paterson, the Convener of the County Council of the joint committee, was quickly on Christian name terms. Provost Annie Mackie of Kilmarnock openly admitted she was in love with him! John had an extraordinary knack of making ordinary people feel at ease and give of their best. He had a great sense of fun. When opening his speech after a lunch prior to a joint committee meeting he complained that the gentleman on his right, Bob Lambie, had not only lambasted his ancestors throughout the lunch but had also eaten his bread roll!

On another occasion. when I was driving him back to Culzean, he insisted, against my plea, we should drive the wrong way round the newly-created one-way system – 'I am, after all, the Chairman!' When met by an opposing car he looked at me and said, 'What are you going to do about it?' Typical!

When Prince Charles was to visit Culzean in 1977, the Queen's Silver Jubilee year, the police security people demanded the castle be 'searched and sealed' prior to the visit and closed to the public. John backed me without further ado, recommending me to take no action. He was always ready with help, advice and support in any situation.

Tom Parkinson

John took me to the gardens at Brodick Castle on Arran, where his easy knowledge and charm blended magically with the beauty and mystery of the place. It was a day I have cherished over the years.

I vividly remember escaping my first Edinburgh haar (a word I suspect originated in a British elision of the word horror), riding at exhilarating speed beside the best driver I have ever encountered. John was the only driver with whom I felt totally relaxed. No wonder that Johnny is so good.

Alex Paulin

John and I first met through the National Trust for Scotland nearly thirty years ago: it was to be another five years before we were on Christian name terms. Our first get together was not smooth, to say the least of it! The Culzean Appeal under his leadership was having a rough time and I found on my arrival at the Trust that the place was in chaos. It was not surprising that John, who at that stage knew little of the background, was highly critical of what he thought were my efforts (they weren't) until, when asked about Culzean, I riposted by saying 'What and where is Culzean?' He understood then that I found that the straight response to him the best road to follow. In all my dealings with him I found this to be so.

Our friendship ripened slowly. I remember the first breaking of the ice was when I was appointed a sort of dog's body to a 'think tank' which included the brightest and best in the Trust – including John. Without thinking I commented on the quality of this lot and John was obviously pleased to be included and to be treated as 'one of the boys'. From this I appreciated for the first time that an ancient lineage and wealthy background can result in the so-called beneficiary being placed on a pedestal, resulting in restricted social access. John was going through a period of isolation and, in his own way, was lonely. Such, combined with a natural diffidence, set him apart. In addition he had to combat a horror of public speaking and I often watched his inner agony on such occasions. But he beat back his nerves and went on to triumph. I saluted him, for a shy man such encounters must have been hell. Courage!

There are two examples of his humility which I treasure and which follow on from my previous points.

The first related to one of the many 'restructurings' that the Trust went through. I countered and disagreed with having a typists' pool, which John thought would be a good idea. I explained that, particularly with senior secretaries, they got to know the eccentricities of their principals and this plus their status enhanced their working attitudes. John, soon in agreement, quietly said to me, 'I quite understand, Alex, but you see I have never worked in an office.' The other instance, more humorous, was when John was signing letter after letter, still without complaint, but writer's cramp was obviously setting in. Iain Atholl, in the Chairman's room at the time, stopped his little libation to say 'I don't think that you have anything to complain about, John. After all, you are only a four-letter word!' John enjoyed that – so did I.

It was around then that we began to address each other informally and the ruderies started. The pedestal was being shattered and some, very few, of the staff followed suit; and I believe that John really enjoyed all this. Certainly he responded – his 'rude postcards' were evidence of this, as were his many invitations of hospitality in Edinburgh, London and elsewhere. He was a very generous and convivial host and badinage flew on such occasions. I enjoyed myself in his company; but it was never easy to return hospitality. However, I managed to on several occasions and I am glad that I did so. At such times, we really explored common ground, just a few of his many interests, each tackled in his inimitable way.

One of my most abiding memories of John, showing his sensitivity and understanding, was over the sadness of Caroline's too premature death. We in the Trust were very fond of her and I found great difficulty in expressing my sympathies in writing to him. I wrote to him and said so, adding that I would miss her too, for I was very fond of her. Within a few days he wrote to me expressing appreciation of my writing and finished up by saying, 'Don't worry, Alex, I can tell you that she was fond of you.' In this way, in my book, he qualified in the humanities.

Francesca *Pelizzoli*

John invited me to Mount Stuart to explore his idea of painting some murals in the Family Corridor. On the first day of my visit he took me on a safari around the Isle of Bute during which we went for a stroll down to a wild beach overlooking Arran. As usual he was impeccably dressed with a high shine on his shoes. The tide was going out and banks of sand were emerging like islands. I could see John was intent on reaching one of those distant points. To my surprise, polished brogues and all, he began striding resolutely through the ankle-deep water. This episode gave me an insight into his personality in the brief period I was to know him.

John's deep attachment to the Isle of Bute and his feelings for Mount Stuart made it important for him to show me the spirit of the place before actually introducing me to the Corridor where I was to work for the next two years.

On and off during this period I learned to recognise his step without turning from my painting and learned also to expect some playful comment or gentle dig. When working on the most awkward corners of the walls, huddled up on the floor, he would invariably sail through remarking that he had caught me asleep on the job again or else he would remind me to lay out my cloth cap. His confidence and encouragement in others' endeavours was an inspiration to me as, I am sure, it was also to other artists and craftsmen who worked on his multitude of projects.

Only someone of John's vision could have conceived of the idea of choosing a book illustrator to be a muralist. He was a true patron of the arts and I feel honoured to have played some part in realising his concept for Mount Stuart.

[95]

Mary Pendreigh

I remember an incident one evening when I was walking towards the Purple Library and Lord Bute jumped out from behind a pillar in the Marble Hall with a glass in his hand and said, 'Boo!', thinking it was Lady Bute. He was very apologetic and I retreated fast, saying, 'It's all right, it's all right. . .'

Another time I had forgotten to lay out Lord Bute's pyjamas, so I telephoned the house at evening dinner time asking for John [Hill]. Lord Bute answered the telephone and confirmed that it was 'John' speaking, and then I realised and got confused (blushing madly). I said I wanted to ask John Hill to lay out the pyjamas as I had forgotten. Lord Bute said, 'It's all right, Mary, I'll put the pyjamas out.'

Another time I was in the Horoscope bathroom cleaning. I heard a noise and asked, 'Who's there?' There was no answer, so I said 'Can you bluidy well no answer?'; and then I saw it was Lord Bute, who just smiled.

Andrew Percy

You will have read, no doubt, in the surrounding pieces of John's Scottish passions, his generous patronage and his elusive wit. What I will remember John most for are the qualities of his gentlemanly demeanour and his real Britishness. I think of him as the last British nobleman.

Without his example I don't think I would know what it means to be 'British', rather than English, Scottish, Welsh or Irish. With his heart in Scotland, his head in London and his forebears in Wales and Ireland, I have never known anyone with such an evenly distributed heritage throughout the isles. I remember the disappointment I felt one evening at Mount Stuart when I baited him with the perfect opportunity to berate the evils of Westminster's remoteness and he responded in measured tones only about the foibles of the institution of the Scottish Office. So often it was what he left unsaid that delivered his message.

His deliberate responses were typical of him – you could have

In a traditional ryokan in Koyto, February 1985.

Canoeing on the lake at Castle Forbes, staying with his uncle, Lord Granard, May 1985.

Opening of 'The Enterprising Scot' in the Royal Scottish Academy, 7 August 1986: with Gus Macdonald.

September 1986. Photograph taken by Grania Cavendish: 'I knew it was really you he had his eye on all along . . .' Sailing round the Turkish coast with Hugh and Grania Cavendish and Mark and Arabella Lennox-Boyd.

Easter 1987. On *King Duck*. John's typical response when Jennifer wanted to photograph him.

Summer 1987, Scandinavia. Sailing round the Danish isles on *King Dick*. Two wicked men enjoying themselves – John and Michael Kennedy breakfasting on deck.

Summer 1987, Sweden. Like the 3rd Earl, 'a very good leg for a boot'.

August 1987. John Home-Rigg, Jennifer and guess who. . . .

August 1987. The visit of the Prince and Princess of Wales (Duke and Duchess of Rothesay) to the Highland Games, Rothesay, Isle of Bute.

February 1988. Monsoon season, Tari, Solomon Islands.

King Duck, May 1988.

May 1988. John's
bonfire on
Colonsay (see
Euan Strathcona's
story).

John semaphoring,
June 1988.

Udaipur, India; with Caroline Beaufort.

Entering the fort (see Caroline Beaufort's story).

followed him for a month, transcribing every word he uttered, and would never have found an ill-considered word or unbalanced sentiment. Perhaps your only objection may have been to his toilet humour when relaxed (a sure sign that he was enjoying himself) and even that is so British!

I say 'last' because he was really out of time. John embodied universal qualities of integrity, respect and honour that somehow became unfashionable as he grew up. He was raised in a manner that had not changed for a hundred years and yet was extinct as soon as he passed through it. A rarefied environment of great wealth and austerity, of great excess and heavy constraint; all of which served to fashion a man of impenetrable self-restraint and impeccable dignity.

That is not to say that John was a man of the past – far from it. He embraced the new with the confidence only available to one who understood his roots. He revelled in modern artistry and was cheered by new social ideas. In fact, I don't know anyone else so open to contemporary art and so willing to fight for space to give it breathing room. His differences over the National Museum design only served to demonstrate the uncertainty others felt about their cultural heritage.

Which brings me to 'nobleman'. John embodied the very essence of nobility. The following is direct from *Roget's Thesaurus*: '*gentleman*, man of probity, man of honour, man of his word, sound character, true man ...', 'square-shooter, true knight, chevalier, galantuomo, caballero, Galahad ...', 'fair player, good loser, sportsman ...', 'Briton; trump, brick ...', 'good sport, true-penny.' You don't have to skip a single word to describe John.

Perhaps the most enduring quality of a really noble man is that he inspires others to reach higher in their pursuit of quality and honour; and so it is with John. That anyone would compare me with him at the end of my life would satisfy me completely.

Diana Percy

While I was living in Jordan I inherited a very battered copy of the *I Ching*, an ancient Chinese oracle (known as the *Book of Changes*). Although far from its traditional sphere of influence, this particular copy had been well used and seemed to possess an appropriate wealth of experience within its pages.

Feeling that there are no rules about the questions one can put to this oracle, and with this piece in mind, I asked about John. The reading I came up with was:

Tui – The Joyous. The attribute of the yielding or dark principle is not joy but melancholy. However, joy is indicated by the fact that there are two strong lines within, expressing themselves through the medium of gentleness. The joy, therefore, rests on firmness and strength within, manifesting itself outwardly as yielding and gentle. The joyous mood is successful and therefore brings success. But joy must be based on steadfastness if it is not to degenerate into uncontrolled mirth.

Truth and strength must dwell in the heart, while gentleness reveals itself in social intercourse. In this way one assumes the right attitude towards God and Man and achieves something. Under certain conditions, intimidation without gentleness may achieve something momentarily but not for all time. When, on the other hand, the hearts of men are won by friendliness, they are led to take all hardships upon themselves willingly, and if need be will not shun death itself, so great is the power of joy over men.

The passage seemed perfectly to encompass something of John's spirit. John possessed a certain 'Orientalness' of spirit: his capacity for wisdom and serenity, his graceful and impeccable style of dress with the attention to detail, the 'courageous tie', all so seemingly unlaboured. He was drawn to the simplicity and discipline in many forms of Oriental art, and though I never witnessed it I could easily have envisaged him with my mother, in the 1980s, practising the meditative martial art of Tai 'Chi on the lawn at Mount Stuart House.

John was involved in so many varied undertakings and interests. I once asked my mother what John actually did, since when the same question was put to me I could only come up with the obvious chairmanships etc. She confessed she didn't altogether know herself, but he was always busy.

Despite so many responsibilities he always seemed to have time to spend with people, without making them feel they were in any way taking up his time. I know of no other person who seemed to be so universally respected and admired.

Richard Percy

I will never forget an occasion when John managed to maintain his poise and sense of humour, though I suspect his pride may have been gently dented, when we were skiing in Andermatt in 1976.

At the end of each day the ski instructors and lift operators would check that all the slopes were clear of people by starting at the uppermost slopes and sweeping their way down to the valley. On this particular afternoon we were amongst the last to be skiing down when the operators caught up with us and watched with incredulity as John patiently attempted to traverse his way down, with these chaps literally breathing down our necks. After a few minutes of *ad hoc* instruction and encouragement, they obviously decided that if they were going to get us down to the valley before dark, they would need to do something that was a little more helpful. So they called on their radios for a stretcher and, when this arrived, they removed John's skis, cajoled him onto the 'blood wagon' and strapped him down. The operators assured him that this was the best and most humane way to descend! We all then skied down with John looking most relieved, if a little embarrassed. What was most admirable was that he took it on the chin, and we all had a good laugh at the bottom.

There was, however, another 'sport' in which John excelled. Bonfires. He just loved bonfires. Any excuse to sweep the beach and collect not just sticks and logs, but bottles, washed-up parking cones, plastic sheets and, of course, his favourite item, rubber tyres – anything and everything was game for this extremely enthusiastic pyromaniac. The bigger (and more aromatic) the fire, the happier he was, and I remember spending many a summer evening watching thick palls of smoke drifting into the effervescent sky from his crackling pyre.

John was extremely fond of *King Duck*, his best-loved 'toy', and often seemed his happiest while entertaining aboard. Trips onto the nearby islands were always *de rigueur*, and one time I was with him as we walked on Lunga. About fifty yards behind us was Giles Kirby,

[99]

who suddenly let out a torrent of expletives. We turned round to see what the commotion was about, only to see Giles scampering among the large rocks behind us for no apparent reason. Then we realised that Giles had inadvertently disturbed a skua's nest and was being dive-bombed in full Stuka style by this very peeved and hostile bird. Try as he might, Giles seemed incapable of escaping these relentless aerial assaults which were aimed straight at his head and had him diving for cover amongst the rocks every few steps. By now John and I were rolling around in hysterics while the expletives exploded from this very agitated man. The more he ducked and darted around the boulders, the more determined and accurate the skua appeared to become. Eventually Giles made it out of the danger zone and showed us the wounds the bird had inflicted on his head – and he had to be bandaged up when we got back to *King Duck*. As I recall, John personally thought the best remedy for him was a large, very stiff drink and a tin helmet in future.

Above all, I remember John as being immensely kind, considerate and generous, and these qualities were always very apparent. Two small examples were when he invited me to take *King Duck*, with my friends, for a week one summer, which was just wonderful, and every winter he would let me have my own weekend shooting parties. He had a marvellously wicked sense of humour as well, which was illustrated by, amongst other things, his butter pats on the high ceiling of the main dining room, his postcards and his mischievous and ambiguous wit. Do I remember him moaning about someone sitting in starvation corner who took hours again to eat his food? Not I!

David Perth

John's great-grandmother was my great-aunt. I remember her clearly and our drives together in London in her electric brougham. I have known well all the succeeding generations. John carried on magnificently his family's tradition of saving Scotland's heritage. Sadly his outstanding work was never recognised by an honour until a few months before he died. In a sense this was his own fault for he never sought publicity, rather he accomplished great things by leading, as it were, from behind. He knew what was right, knew what he wanted and got it – the iron fist in the velvet glove. All who knew him and worked with him enjoyed his sense of fun, his quiet modesty offset by sparkling sartorial ventures.

I saw much of him these last years as we worked together on his last and greatest challenge – the new Museum of Scotland. It was a project I had very much at heart and had worked for. John knew this and several years ago I got a letter in his small, neat hand asking if I would join his team and head the Appeal. I couldn't resist John and the challenge. These last years have confirmed his skills in getting things done despite the complexities of the task and despite the perils of bureaucracy. He knew his way in the corridors of power though never a politician.

I recall the awkward and embarrassing event of several years ago when the Prince of Wales, having become President of the Patrons for the Appeal, resigned just before the outcome of the international architectural competition was announced. I have no intention of going into the whys and wherefores of that event though I dare to believe that none of us were blameless. The awkward fact was that, owing to a chapter of accidents, the resignation leaked the day before we were having a press conference to announce the winners of the competition for the new building. What to do? John was sad but calm and determined to go through with the conference.

There was a large turn out of the Press, not to learn the result but to ask why the Prince had resigned. John had warned me that after announcing the winners (Benson and Forsyth, a small firm based in London with its partners from Newcastle and Glasgow), he intended to pass me the answering of the resignation questions – masterly delegation! I dealt with them as best I could without attaching any blame or exacerbating things. John's typical comment after the conference I remember well: 'We couldn't have gained better publicity for the new museum!'

Since then building plans have gone steadily forward, John at the centre of it all. He organised the many committees needed for such a complicated task, choosing the right experts and presiding wherever needed. He trusted his chosen team and let them get on with the job.

In these last years he was tragically stricken with cancer but it made little difference to him and all his work. Supported by Jennifer, he courageously carried on with quiet humour and efficiency to oversee progress, and before he died he knew that things inexorably would go on to completion despite the economic depression.

All this time John and Jennifer went on with the restoration and completion of Mount Stuart and its gardens – her courage and comfort the equal of his. And so the family home will survive and, together with the new museum, be fitting monuments to his achievement – the betterment of Scotland.

Jeremy Pilcher

From astonishment on first being shown Mount Stuart by John over forty years ago, to a last elegiac visit with him to favourite places on Bute, memories of his kindness, humour, wide interests and courage will be imperishable. Others will doubtless write on the last two of these qualities, so apparent later in his life. The following stories may serve to exemplify the two former which so impressed themselves on me.

I do not think I was the only young guest at Mount Stuart to have been a little daunted by the first evening at dinner. But any such apprehension we might have had was soon dispelled by the sporadic plop of butter pats from the remote ceiling (flicked there by John and his brothers and now softened by the heat of so many candles) and by the delighted reaction of John and his family when one landed in the hair of an older guest.

Nor did John's humour desert him when, in the mists of the following afternoon, two or three of the younger guns shot at (but fortunately missed) a greenshank in mistake, so they said, for a great snipe. John told the guilty parties of his father's love of ornithology and that people had been sent home for less, but soon transformed the effect by roaring with laughter at the first signs of their discomfort.

These anecdotes, though trivial in themselves, still serve to remind me of the beginning of my lifelong friendship with John.

Meredith Pilcher

John Donne was wrong when he wrote 'no man is an island' for if anyone was an island, *genius loci*, that man was John Bute.

He loved his island with its many different landscapes and views.

The solid architecture of the Victorian marine villas on the road from Rothesay, the long sweep of the moorlands, the craggy hills and the shallow valleys falling down to the long sea views. He loved the tiny bays, bordered with sea pink and lavender and the special pinkish mushrooms which grew in the upland fields. His island was his home, his fortress. It was his memories and it is his memorial.

In many ways John was very like his island. He could sometimes seem separated from the mainland of his fellow creatures; a remote, self-contained being. At other times, like the island, he was drawn gladly into the commerce of humanity, especially relishing and contributing to its more humorous aspects.

The last time I saw him, on the Whitsun weekend three months before he died, John spent most of these brief last days together driving myself and the others who stayed that weekend, round the island to show us places and views we had, perhaps, never seen before. And also, I suspect, to take farewell of those views himself.

He drove us high up on the moors, over sheep tracks and along secret, sunken drovers' roads, right to the top of the island to see a particular view of the sea to the west and Arran. We went to look at the ruined chapel and climbed high on the hills above it; we visited an empty farmhouse for which he was busily making plans for restoration and we had a lively debate on architecture while he showed us round the Landmark Trust restoration of a seventeenth-century house in which one of his uncles had once lived.

Late on the Saturday afternoon he and I went on an outing to Rothesay to collect his medicine. On our way back he took me to look at the family mausoleum behind Rothesay ('rather grim, don't you think?') and then he drove me down to the sea to look at the earlier family graveyard which was, at that time, still surrounded by a wall. Didn't I think that it would be nicer if the wall was pulled down, he asked. I agreed.

And then we went back to Mount Stuart for tea.

John Ramsay

Though I saw John on a fairly regular basis at Trustees' meetings of the Columba Trust during the last ten years of his life, the time I saw most of him was many years before that when we served together in

[103]

the 1st Battalion Scots Guards at Golfcourse Camp, Port Said, in the Canal Zone between January 1952 and December 1954.

To those of us who had been in the battalion since it was re-formed in the summer of 1951, Port Said was just another camp, but to a young officer like John, coming out with a draft from England, it must have been a rude shock. 'Golfcourse Camp' was not as it sounds: in fact it looked remarkably like a POW camp, having a fifteen-foot-high reinforced barbed-wire perimeter fence.

Looking back at that time, I can recall no incident involving John in particular. You might think that this meant he never made his mark. You would be quite wrong. The only ones one does recall are those individuals who 'bogged it' in some way or other... In other words, John adapted happily and easily to battalion life. Doubtless it was during this time that he developed the talent that was so conspicuous in his later years, of being completely at his ease in any kind of company and of making others feel equally at home with him.

Life was dull and monotonous: drill, weapon training and 'Interior Economy' – a glorious military term covering anything from darning your socks to whitewashing the walls of the company office. There were rare excursions when a company would go off on detachment to the Red Sea hills for shooting practice and our tents were pitched close to the seashore with the precious opportunity of bathing among the coral reefs. Some of us, too, managed to do a little sailing in and around Port Said harbour. Then there were the occasional visits to the Akri Palace Hotel, the Penthouse Restaurant of which overlooked the harbour; there one dined on prawns that were larger and more succulent and delicious than any I have ever eaten since. One tried not to think what the prawns had fed on, since they came straight out of the harbour.

The greater part of the time, however, was very dreary and so any and every opportunity was taken to have a party. With Port Said harbour close by, there were periodic visits by vessels of the Royal Navy so there was no shortage of people to entertain.

What did we *achieve*? People talk nowadays of a 'police presence' where the constabulary are *seen* but not necessarily *heard*. That perhaps is the reason we were there – providing a presence to deter troublemakers. Certainly, for the three years we were there, there was no trouble and though we ourselves were bored to tears, the fact that there was peace was no small achievement.

John taken by Lucy Lambton, October 1989.

Bute Pipe Band at Mount Stuart, Christmas 1989.

King Duck, June 1990. In Ireland with Diana Percy and the crew – Jim Fisher (skipper) and Ken Scott (engineer).

Dumfries House.

John's mother, Eileen, the late Dowager Marchioness of Bute, with her grandson Johnny Dumfries, at the christening of Johnny's son, Jack, at Dumfries House, 25 August 1990.

Summer 1991: in the Wee Garden at Mount Stuart with Chris Page and Martin Gardner of the Royal Botanic Gardens, Edinburgh.

John communicated by card. These fell through letter boxes full of thanks, remembering promises, or just to amuse. The latter, to close friends, were highly prized, private and often outrageous, but never offensive. The cards were carefully collected in desk drawers. The two illustrated here are a mild reminder – one to Stephen Gibbs and the other to John's granddaughter Samantha Bain.

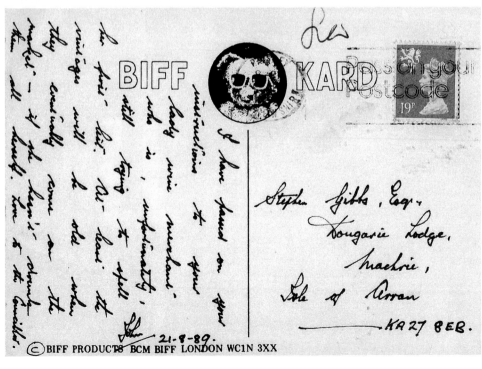

The card to Samantha Bain.

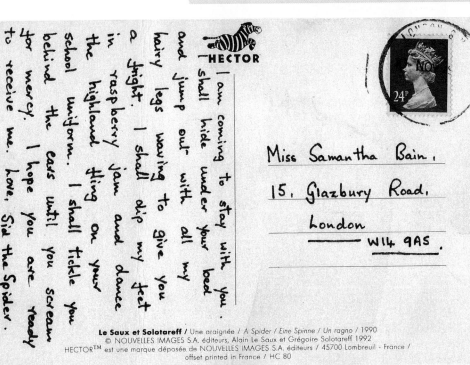

HECTOR

I am coming to stay with you. I shall hide under your bed and jump out with all my hairy legs waving to give you a fright. I shall dip my feet in raspberry jam and dance the highland fling on your school uniform. I shall tickle you behind the ears until you scream for mercy. I hope you are ready to receive me. Love, Sid the Spider.

Miss Samantha Bain,
15, Glazbury Road,
London
———— W14 9AS.

Le Saux et Solotareff / Une araignée / A Spider / Eine Spinne / Un ragno / 1990
© NOUVELLES IMAGES S.A. éditeurs, Alain Le Saux et Grégoire Solotareff 1992
HECTOR™ est une marque déposée de NOUVELLES IMAGES S.A. éditeurs / 45700 Lombreuil - France /
offset printed in France / HC 80

30 May 1991. John as Lord Lieutenant of Bute and Argyll (second time around) on Tiree with HRH The Princess Royal *(Oban Times.)*

June 1993: the last photograph –
outside the family entrance with
Jennifer. Taken by Sally Hardie.

Autumn 1992. National
Museums of Scotland
Trustees meeting to discuss
the new building for the
Museum of Scotland.

One of the murals by
Francesca Pelizzoli
commissioned by
John.

Coat of arms above
the fireplace in
Jennifer's study
devised by Don
Pottinger, Islay
Herald of Arms and
Lyon Clerk and
Keeper of the
Records.

John, like the rest of us, did his dreary job well and without any fuss. Nobody paid us any compliments – after all, what were we doing? Nothing! But I like to think that keeping the peace is *not* nothing. John and the rest of us did not waste our time but developed talents which have stood us in good stead ever since.

Jorge Ross

A friendship that lasted for almost forty years and at a considerable distance from one another (I live in Chile) carries a degree of understanding between two people uncommon in today's frantic living, where friendship is being replaced by meetings mutually convenient.

Whenever we met, usually under very different circumstances, be it skiing at Courchevel or hurrying through New York, when times were favourable or not that favourable, meeting was always a treat and nothing but fond recollections remain.

We were both brought up at Ampleforth, although at different times, and whenever our paths crossed John's standard query would be, 'When are you coming to the island?'

He finally came to Chile with Jennifer. Wine tasting was part of the trip. As we sat at the far end of the table watching Jennifer's expertise, his good-humoured heckling interruptions were a high note of the gathering.

Steven Runciman

Long ago, in 1933, I used now and then to see a double pram emerge from the house next door to my parents' in Westminster. One day it was accompanied by the twins' mother, whom I knew slightly as her brother, Arthur Forbes, later Lord Granard, had been a pupil of mine at Cambridge, a youth whose charming manners almost compensated for his lack of interest in learning. She introduced me to her infant sons. So, when I met John Bute well over thirty years later I could announce myself to be an old friend of his, a claim that he regarded with sceptical amusement but which he was in no position to deny.

I came to know him in the later 1960s, when I came on to the

Executive Committee of the National Trust for Scotland and he soon afterwards became its Chairman. I had given up driving a car by then, a task that I had never enjoyed; and when journeys were necessary he would kindly give me a lift. At first they were silent journeys. He had a driver, which enabled him to immerse himself in the papers that he had to study, while I admired the scenery. Then, after some months, he would interrupt his reading to ask me what I thought about some issue, or to make comments on our colleagues which were shrewd and sometimes critical but never unkind or unjust. During those years I was increasingly impressed by his skill as a chairman. I have known no one else who could so ably and promptly summarise a discussion and who was gifted with such patience and such humour.

During those early years of our acquaintanceship he would never talk about himself. It was only much later, when his own private life was happier, that I came to know him as a warm and charming friend. Many others, I know, will have described the delight of staying with him and Jennifer at Mount Stuart, in that fascinating and eccentric house which they were rehabilitating with such devotion and taste. He was at times a bit autocratic as a host, but benevolent. If I pleaded old age as an excuse for not joining in some energetic expedition, I would be let off with a tolerant smile. I was not unhappy when, staying there once, I had as a fellow guest that other Island Marquess, Henry Anglesey, whose lameness, the result of having been run over by a young lady in a London mews, enabled him to resist John's more strenuous schemes, thus rescuing me from them too. I hope that John derived as much pleasure from these house parties as did his guests.

All good things come to an end; but it is heart-breaking when the end comes painfully and too soon. But, with thousands of others, I am very grateful for the privilege of having known John.

Francis Russell

John's appearance told something of the man: fastidious, yet as the cut of the suits and the courage of the ties indicated, keenly interested in every manifestation of design. His knowledge, lightly worn, was matched by a sense of humour, a taste for the tease which was relished by anyone who experienced this. 'Isn't this a *bugger* of a party!' he might remark, when surrounded by his chosen guests at Mount Stuart. The language was indeed personal. Thus the word 'choice' – used much, but in a rather different sense, by his mother – would express his delight with the most pornographic of postcards.

Anyone who inherits a great estate has perforce to live with the work of his ancestors. John's passion for architecture and gardening were unquestionably inherited. Others are better qualified to relate how his instinctive judgement and strong commitment were deployed in the public service and to record what he achieved at Mount Stuart. I will content myself with two vignettes.

Some years ago Lord Lonsdale told me of a series of drawings of Mount Stuart by the Prime Minister's daughter, Lady Mary Lowther. One of these proved to be the most accurate record of the Hermitage the 3rd Earl built in the policies. When next on Bute, I set off at John's suggestion to look at the site. Poking about with a stick in a heap of overgrown rubble, I surmised that most of the components of the façade might survive. Some months later John suggested that I should have another look. The Hermitage had been restored, using the 3rd Earl's rough, rusticated blocks of local stone, to serve, once again, as the focal point of the long cut through the woods on the foreshore which John had characteristically had the prescience to preserve.

No aspect of construction was too humble to engage John's interest. Some months before he died, Jennifer proposed a picnic on the foreshore. This was littered with debris and John determined to make a bonfire. It was gratifying to see the precision with which he positioned the wood we gathered and the efficiency with which whole piles of plastic were consumed in the resulting furnace. Despite the pain that already made it torture to eat or talk, John seemed and *was* as happy as the proverbial sandboy.

Houston Shaw-Stewart

After one very lengthy and boozy shooting lunch with John on Bute, we all emerged slightly the worse for wear – that is except for Jim M[acdonald]-B[uchanan], who was *much* the worse. The head keeper very politely and gently removed his gun, John smiled, and the shoot proceeded.

Lucinda Shaw-Stewart

I first met John in the mid-Seventies whilst staying with some mutual friends in Northumberland. My first impressions were of his charm, and sense of humour, and his intense – and surprising – shyness. Due to his modesty and reserve I was, at first, unaware of the extraordinary range of his capabilities; these were to unfold themselves to me later. Neither did I sense the remarkable effect that this chance meeting was to have on my own future.

I was soon to work for him as the London representative of the National Trust for Scotland, of which he was then Chairman, and through his typical generosity was given the use of an office in the beautiful house in Queen Anne's Gate, which he used as his own offices. It had been the home of Edward Hudson, founder of *Country Life*, and John worked in the Lutyens-altered dining-room at the back of the house. We always used to imagine all the fruitful article-planning which had taken place over the port in that very room.

At the same stage John and Jennifer asked me to help them sort through the furniture at Mount Stuart as a preliminary to their programme of restoration there. It was a joy to see the Butes at work on this dauntingly huge conservation project, which was to flower in the 1980s into those remarkable commissions through which John and Jennifer were to make their own very special contribution to that great Victorian palace – seeking out new talent and commissioning painters, glass-engravers and stainers, sculptors and gilders to contribute towards its completion in a rare example of late twentieth-century private patronage, fully in the spirit of John's great-grandfather, the building 3rd Marquess. It is particularly painful that John was destined to die before this splendid project reached fruition.

When, in 1982, I married Houston – a lifelong friend and neighbour of John – our ties were further strengthened and though the Mount Stuart work and London job now ceased, my return to the Trust as Council and Executive Committee member involved continuing to work for him. It also gave me the opportunity to witness his extraordinary skill as Chairman and his inspired and inspiring leadership. Under him the Trust expanded, flourished and prospered, and the high esteem in which it came to be held world-wide can really be attributed to the charismatic combination of John as Chairman, David Wemyss as President and Jamie Stormonth Darling as Director in these golden years.

I can picture, once again, the scene in the Adam boardroom of 5 Charlotte Square on Executive Committee days, with John seated at the top table, neat and dapper with the added accent of a very flashy tie, wreathing poor Jamie in clouds of evil-smelling cheroot smoke, as he worked his way elegantly through the agenda. He listened to all viewpoints but steered the meeting with consummate skill, intelligence and humour. His poise was all the more admirable as his twisting of hands and crossing and re-crossing of legs reminded us all of the agony of shyness against which he battled, and which he seems only to have conquered in the last painful months of his life.

No problem seemed insuperable to him; when presented with a tricky challenge he would chuckle and, after thought, come up with the very person who could solve it. His knowledge of the heritage world in Scotland was immense and far-reaching, and one felt that – from some great Olympian height – he was constantly surveying the overall scene, weighing up its strengths and weaknesses, time and again, deftly placing the missing piece in a jigsaw puzzle of which one was only half aware.

Because of John's great modesty I don't think many of his friends realised the full extent of his varied activities until they came to read his obituaries. The gap he leaves is all too painfully apparent in so many organisations, and we must all live with the regret, too, that his dedicated work was inadequately acknowledged in his lifetime, though this is probably as he would have wished.

But for Houston and myself, the memories we shall always treasure are the many laughs we shared together, the happy days spent on *King Duck*, the stream of witty postcards inscribed in his neat hand, and the warmth and generosity of his friendship.

Jimmy Shields

I remember an incident when Lord Bute and his twin brother were young and I was in charge of them and the youngest brother, James, going to a fair in Rothesay and driving the dodgems. Lord Bute and David were being unruly and kept bumping into my dodgem, young James at my side, and were put out of their cars. On our return I was told off by Lord Bute's father for not being able to control the boys, but the Dowager just said to her husband: 'Have you ever been in a dodgem?'

Billy Shields

One evening Lord Bute and two guests were going up in the lift. Anne[1] said that she would come up later. Lord Bute's reply was that if Sir Houston [Shaw-Stewart] and the Captain[2] and I could fit in, it would take her as well. Lord Bute asked which floor she would like to go to. She said, 'Number 4.' The Captain and Lord Bute started to call out the floors, '1 – Toy Department; 2 – Men's Wear; 3 – Ladies' Underwear; 4 – Penthouse.' I've never seen Anne with such a red face.

Lord Bute phoned me up one night and said could I go and 'arrest'[3] a wild dog which was down on the beach. It turned out to be a four-month-old alsatian cross. It took me about three hours to find it, and when I finally did so it had a leg stuck through the deer fence. This dog became a member of the family at Mount Stuart House.

Coming back by Glendaruel in the Mercedes, Lord Bute and Patrick Crichton[4] were in the back. I was behind a coach for some time. Lord Bute said 'Do you think you could show him our exhaust?' At this time I was doing 75 mph. My foot went down on the gas and we passed the coach at about 105 mph. Looking in my rear-view mirror I saw Lord Bute with his eyes closed, relaxed and

1 Housemaid.
2 Michael Lowsley-Williams, John's brother-in-law.
3 Billy was a special constable.
4 Secretary.

lying back in the seat, Mr Crichton was pure white. When we got to the ferry, Mr Crichton excused himself. Lord Bute said, 'Do you think he was a wee bit feart?' and gave a chuckle.

Lord and Lady Bute were returning from a trip on *King Duck*. I was to meet them at the Crinan Hotel. Jim Fisher, the skipper, had brought Lady Bute and Kapelo [her Finnish spitz] by rubber dinghy. Lady Bute jumped, slipped and fell into the sea. Lord Bute said that if Lady Bute had waited, Jim would have taken her safely to dry land. 'Maybe she was just so pleased to see you,' he added.

Robert H. Smith

It was a custom of the National Museums of Scotland Trustees to go away for an 'away weekend' and a few years ago we went to Islay. After a hard day of meetings and visiting local museums and archaeological sites we were given a conducted tour of the Bowmore Distillery. We were each given a miniature Bowmore whisky and offered a free, plastic suit cover which could fairly be described as 'naff', with gilt lettering announcing that we had received it from the Bowmore Distillery. As John Bute rose to go and collect his suit cover I pointed out that not only was he very wealthy but that as a marquess he should demonstrate some standards and refuse to collect his free gift. Quick as a flash he turned to me and said, beaming seraphically, 'Ah, but Robert, it is for my Coronation robes.' Collapse of one stout aristocrat-baiter!

I had been learning a little about portraits and was telling Lord Bute, who was of course a great expert on paintings, that the important things to look for in a portrait were depth and richness of colour and well-painted extremities, that is hands and feet. Good painters can paint portraits well but only geniuses could paint hands and feet adequately. John listened kindly to my rantings and then said very quietly that there were exceptions, such as Frans Hals who, according to John, painted hands like bunches of bananas. Flushed with my new-found knowledge, I recapped, 'So then, John, good portraits have richness of colour and well painted hands and feet with the exception of people like Frans Hals who painted hands like bunches of bananas.' John looked at me sadly for a moment and then said, 'Robert, you *are* a charlatan.'

On another occasion, during John's long illness, I had to deputise on a few occasions and found dealing with a board which is full of very clever and articulate people quite a challenge. John returned for a board meeting shortly before he died. This was held in Edinburgh Castle. One of our Trustees was Sir Nicholas Fairbairn who had strong views against something that John believed in. I wondered how John, who was not at all well, would handle Nicky, in brilliant articulate form, at the meeting. As we were going into the meeting, I saw John put his arm round Nicky's shoulder and heard him say, 'Nicky, I wonder if you would be so good as to speak in favour of this particular item on the agenda?' This happened to be the item that Nicky had been totally opposed to. When we got to the item on the agenda, Nicky stepped in immediately and said, 'Chairman, before you open up discussion on this topic, may I just say something?' He then gave, as only Nicky could, a brilliant and witty speech strongly supporting Lord Bute's proposition, to the dismay and astonishment of his previous supporters who had been opposed to Lord Bute's view. Needless to say, the outcome was resounding support for John.

Gavin Stamp

Abbot Sir David Hunter Blair's biography of the 3rd Marquess of Bute, the builder of Cardiff Castle, reproduced a photograph of that great scholar, mystic and patron of the arts wearing his robes as Rector of the University of St Andrews and looking like a monk. The late John Crichton-Stuart, the 6th Marquess, did not favour medieval dress – although he was something of a dandy – but the physical resemblance to his great-grandfather was uncanny. He had, in middle age, the same heavy jowls and the same melancholy, pouchy eyes. And he was also so like his forebear in his tireless activity on behalf of innumerable good causes, and in his deep concern for the arts and architecture of Scotland.

Although a very rich man, modern circumstances did not permit John Bute to erect new castles and churches or to restore ancient abbeys and cathedrals. Instead, he followed in the footsteps of his grandfather, the 4th Marquess, another munificent benefactor, who was instrumental in the foundation of both the National Trust for Scotland and the National Monuments Record for Scotland. John Bute served successively as Chairman of the Trust and as Chairman of the Historic Buildings Council for Scotland, and was widely admired for his tact and effectiveness in both roles. He had, indeed, a vision for and of Scotland which, sadly, is not sufficiently shared by many of his compatriots.

Like his predecessors, John Bute was always ready to support another good cause. I was delighted and relieved to have his encouragement when I founded the Alexander Thomson Society [in 1991]. He knew all about Glasgow and had long been concerned about the neglect of its historic architecture. The saving of Thomson's finest villa, Holmwood, was a cause close to his heart and he was working quietly, behind the scenes, to get it into the hands of the National Trust for Scotland even during his terrible final illness. If we succeed in this, the restoration of Holmwood would be a fitting memorial to him.

Nor was John Bute only concerned with historic architecture. He was the moving force behind the competition for a prominent new extension to the Museum of Scotland in Edinburgh – won by the Anglo-Scottish partnership, Benson and Forsyth, with an unashamedly Corbusian design. And when the Prince of Wales misguidedly attempted to interfere, as he did not sympathise with the decisions of the assessors, Lord Bute was not in the least intimidated – he was, after all, of Royal Stuart descent himself, and an earlier Lord Bute had been Prime Minister to the young George III as well as a patron of Robert Adam. John Bute's concern with both good design and with Scottish industries led to the establishment of Bute Fabrics and, like the 3rd and 4th Marquesses, he was greatly interested in tapestry weaving – only a tawdry economy by Government has prevented his company supplying a large modern tapestry to help redeem the interior of the new British Library in London.

John Bute's deep sense of duty and public service came from consciousness of his lineage. I first met him when he asked me to write about Robert Weir Schultz, the Arts and Crafts architect who had worked for both his great-grandfather and grandfather, and so I had the privilege of visiting Mount Stuart, the colossal Gothic

Revival house hidden away on the Isle of Bute and designed by Rowand Anderson for the amazing 3rd Marquess, which had long been a legend amongst enthusiasts for Victorian architecture. I was not disappointed: it was a glorious, mysterious, introverted pile with a central arcaded marble hall dimly lit by astrological stained glass. It was also then, in the mid-1970s, rather melancholy – like its owner, who was then contemplating leaving the house as he 'rather rattled around in it' (something of an understatement).

At heart a very shy man, John Bute was funny but had much sadness in his private life – and there was more to come. But everything was transformed at Mount Stuart when he married, as his second wife, Jennifer Percy. The new Marchioness set about making it look as its creators had intended, and decorative schemes that had been abandoned when the 3rd Marquess died in 1900 were resumed. It was wonderful to see this great intractable house come alive and see how happy John Bute was there in recent years. But a sense of melancholy remained. Although he bore his cruelly disfiguring cancer with astonishing dignity and inspiring courage – never permitting it to interfere with his many enterprises – one felt he knew his time had come.

The 2nd Marquess, who recouped the family's fortunes by developing Cardiff Docks, died suddenly at the age of 55. His son, the 3rd Marquess, who turned his back on the Industrial Revolution and became a mediaevalist and a Roman Catholic, died at only 53. The great efforts to save historic Scottish architecture by the shy and retiring 4th Marquess were impeded by illness before he died in 1947 at 65 and his son, John's father, died at the age of 49. John Bute survived his mother by a fortnight; he had managed to reach 60 before going to join his ancestors by the little eighteenth-century church by the sea at Mount Stuart. His departure leaves an appalling void in the architectural and cultural life of Scotland. [Published in the *Spectator*, 31 July 1993.]

Jamie Stormonth Darling

THE NATIONAL TRUST FOR SCOTLAND

For thirty-seven years of his tragically short life – he died soon after his sixtieth birthday (27 February 1993) on 21 July 1993 – he had devoted so much of his thought and time to the National Trust for Scotland. He was following a family tradition. His grandfather made a special plea for the rehabilitation of Scotland's vernacular architecture, advocating massive sums being given to the Trust soon after it was founded in 1931. His father bequeathed St Kilda, which forty years later – in 1987 – was declared the first World Heritage site in Scotland.

It was no wonder therefore that John was elected to the Council of the Trust in 1964 and appointed to be its Chairman five years later – a leadership which the Trust enjoyed for fifteen years, and which continued when he was elected President until his death.

His first overt, and outstanding, initiative in Council was to negotiate that the Trust become the owner of Nos 5, 6 and 7 Charlotte Square, Edinburgh. This far-sighted and generous decision, taken in the face of tempting offers by institutions, has resulted in residences for the Secretary of State for Scotland and the Moderator of the General Assembly of the Church of Scotland; a Georgian house open to the public and the Trust as rightful owner – and not tenant – of No. 5.

The Trust's status rose to new heights under his leadership thanks to his wisdom in determining policy and in decision-making; to his wide knowledge of art, architecture, gardens and everything to do with the countryside; to his wit as a public speaker on committees; and above all to his deep and sincere interest and concern for every individual. This last and great quality was fully appreciated by everyone with whom John came into contact, whatever their background in life.

THE MUSEUM OF SCOTLAND

John's magnificently wide vision for the future of the Museum of Scotland has made its enduring mark on the nation. His unbounded enthusiasm was also deeply engraved on individuals like Mary and me. He invited us, in all innocence, to a fund-raising dinner and auction in the Museum. A slightly guilty conscience that we should be so well cared for was soon dispelled when the auction came to the original and only edition of A. O. Curle's most learned treatise on the Traprain Treasure. I muttered to Mary that I really ought to make a bid since our house at Dirleton looks straight across the fertile fields of East Lothian to Traprain and we delight in its ever-changing lights and shades. (Perhaps John overheard this rash suggestion.)

It was on Traprain's western shoulder that this unique cache of Roman silver was discovered in 1919. When the bidding raced beyond £50, I took fright. Without ever being guilty of a wink or a nod, I vainly tried to see who was bidding against whom. Both parties were obviously well practised and the duel ended at £110. The auctioneer looked at John, who immediately announced 'Stormonth Darling' as the successful bidder, then turned to me sitting behind him and said, 'I felt it was only appropriate that you should own this book so that every time you look out of your window you will remember this occasion.' He was right, but it was a sure test of friendship when I wrote out that cheque.

CULZEAN AND ITS COUNTRY PARK

John had greatly loved Culzean for nearly thirty years in his service to the Trust. It was the first country park in Scotland, and it set a pattern for others throughout the UK. It was a marvellously happy example of cooperation between the Trust and the neighbouring local authorities.

In 1979 a guest of honour was required at the celebration of its first ten years. As Her Majesty Queen Elizabeth, The Queen Mother, was the Trust's patron as well as the grandmother of the Earl of Carrick, her name was naturally suggested. During a pause in an animated discussion, Provost Annie Mackie of Kilmarnock intervened: 'With no disrespect of any kind to Her Majesty, whom we all admire tremendously, Mr Chairman, *I just want John Bute.*'

When the great day came, after the speeches, Bill Paterson as Convener of Ayr County Council and therefore Chairman of the Country Park, formally attired and wearing a highly polished top hat, mounted his carriage to steer his pair of horses through the park with Provost Annie and, of course, John Bute. A surreptitious tap on Provost Anne's shoulder and a conspiratorial whisper, 'You have your John Bute now'; and off they went, only to require pushing up the hill from the Visitor Centre. There are some good photographs at Culzean to confirm this happy scene.

POSTCARDS

Who could rival John in that combination of wisdom, humour,

observation and economy of words, whether he was replying to some urgent – probably complicated – issue or on holiday observing the nationals of other countries? But it was usually the subject matter or substance of the postcard which was more eagerly studied than his writings – original though they were. However, on one occasion his neat hand conveyed a serious threat. During those happy years when John was the Trust's Chairman, the practice was that the Director's expenses should be approved by 'Himself'. The Director (myself) – or as he sometimes purposely said in public, the 'Dictator', only to correct himself with an immediate apology – was often late in submitting his expense claim. I received a particularly interesting postcard in an envelope. Turning it over – reluctantly – I read: 'If you do not send me your note on expenses at once, the next postcard will reach you for all the staff to see. I am getting very short of envelopes.'

DODO V ALIAS *KING DUCK*

During a wonderfully carefree and happy children's cruise in our early days, when John and young Johnny, aged ten, played host to our teenage son and daughter and a visiting French boy, we were puzzled by Johnny habitually calling his father 'Mons'. After many games of Vingt et Un and happy visits to Rum and Skye (Loch Coruisk) it emerged that 'Mons' was short for 'Monster'. Maybe it had started pejoratively, but by that cruise it had clearly become a term of the warmest affection – and John scolded me for not instructing son Angus to call him 'John'. We all remember that cruise as a week of sheer enchantment, filled with love and laughter.

Euan Strathcona

The Butes' visit to Colonsay in 1991 left an indelible memory. Our friends were impressed at the arrival of the splendid historic yacht *King Duck*, altogether the dignity of the occasion was somewhat tarnished when one of the crew put his backside through a saloon window as they came alongside the pier. Ship repair facilities are inevitably limited on Colonsay. However, we were able to cut a piece of plywood which made a seamanlike, if somewhat primitive, temporary repair. John, meanwhile, emerged his usual immaculate self.

The triumph of the visit was highlighted by his impeccable turnout, to which we are hardly accustomed on Colonsay. The wearing of ties, for example, is ordinarily limited to island weddings and funerals. At first John maintained his dapper appearance, even when tending the inevitable bonfire – we were clearing the woodland garden of the encroaching jungle of ponticum rhododendron. Then we noticed that he would disappear from time to time and return looking mysteriously satisfied. On the last afternoon, the truth was revealed. John was discovered busily stoking the fire – without his tie! We have a photograph to prove it. But it was only a temporary victory. As *King Duck* sailed away, bearing the battle scar of the patched window, John was once again immaculate.

Stewart Tod

My first meeting with the Marquess of Bute was fifteen years ago at a Planning Conference when I disagreed with an outspoken critic of the then Conservation Grant system, as my experience of the HBC was very different. John Bute, whom I did not know at the time, replied to the critic with a very positive response, gently delivered but precise and final.

It was more than five years later that I became closely involved in the programme of upgrading Mount Stuart and I learned that my earlier meeting with John Bute was typical. His manner was gentle, easy and sometimes whimsical, yet positive when guidance on a design point was sought.

The fun and enjoyment of the work we were doing was ever-present. The design he inspired at a fireplace, incomplete since the end of the nineteenth century, produced carvings of a large cat on the right of the fireplace staring impotently at mice playing happily a few feet away on the left. This streak of fun continues the tradition set by the 3rd Marquess in tiny carvings of birds, insects, flowers and animals – nearly one hundred of them around his bedroom.

The bed designed in 1992 to complete this room was first drawn with a bold lion perched on the tester. The quiet fun appeared again and the lion was transformed, appropriately, into a sleepy fellow with a night cap slipping off, peering down to the bedposts where Badger on the pipes is preparing to accompany Reynard with a psaltery.

John Bute was inspirational in his instructions and he gave numerous carvers, artists, glass-workers and metal-workers opportunities to produce works of art. His own house will ultimately be discreetly sprinkled with tiny bees (for Bute) in paint, ceramic, stone, bronze or wood to indicate those sections of the house finally completed by him, as his signature. No bland system of dates would satisfy him.

His love of Bute will one day be expressed in stone with a carving he planned for the Port-Cochère at the main entrance to the house. He chose the passage from Dryden's *Tempest* previously used by the 2nd Earl of Bute for his garden doorway:

> Henceforth this isle to the afflicted be
> A place of refuge, as it was to me;
> The promises of blooming spring live here,
> And all the blessings of the ripening year.

John has 'only slipped away into the next room' and one day there should be yet another 'bee' beside the carving.

Rosemary Verey

It was a special moment in my life when John and Jennifer invited me to Mount Stuart. Working on his house, woodland and policies, he still found time and inspiration for a less glamorous part of his estate. In the nineteenth century an ancestress had begun to create a walled vegetable garden, as was the fashion in Victorian times. John, with his eclectic historical interest, decided to carry on where she had left off.

This is where I came in, in the autumn of 1990, and on each visit John's enthusiasm took hold of me. There have been Earls or Marquesses of Bute at Rothesay since the eighteenth century. The 3rd Earl guided Princess Augusta, wife and widow of Frederick Prince of Wales, in the early development of Kew Gardens – especially the physic garden and arboretum – during its formative years in the mid eighteenth century. The 3rd Earl may have equalled John's prowess but surely did not surpass his vision and love of Mount Stuart, of the Scottish landscape, its history and art and its future.

John was a mixture of being supremely gentle but at the same time essentially forceful. He held you in a state of animated suspense. I loved the way that after I had made a radical suggestion he would pause, and I would wonder if he had been thinking of something else. Then, sure enough, a change would come over his face, first quizzical, then thoughtful, and eventually I would hear his reaction. I loved to walk with him and Jennifer in the garden around the house as it was illuminating to learn about the shrubs and trees that his family had planted over the centuries, always chosen to suit the ecology and climate of the west coast. John felt, and he conveyed in a subtle, almost unspoken way, that he was a link in an unbroken chain between past and future generations.

John was incapable of being dull, whether discussing plans for the potager, when he would emphasise the importance of culinary herbs as well as those for medicine, or at dinner when flashes of amusement would light up his face as he invited you to taste Jennifer's delicious wine before sharing with you his latest schemes.

These visits to Mount Stuart will live for ever in my mind as an echo of past grandeur, glimpses of how our Victorian ancestors survived in a cold castle and how John had made it his life's work to bring his ancestral home up to twentieth-century comfort. John was a visionary, forever looking to the future, fascinated by the huge challenge which lay ahead of him and the future generations of his family. He was a wonderful friend.

Kay Watt

Friendship with John was a voyage of discovery, there were so many facets to his personality and for me the most fascinating were the contrasts.

As a host he could be gravely charming and maddeningly cheeky almost in the same breath: 'How lovely of you to come, may I get you a drink? – For heaven's sake! Would you have a decent whisky before you turn into a bloody Coca Cola.' He wore the most quietly elegant suits, and teamed them with dazzling ties. He could be impeccably correct, conforming to the rules with flawless courtesy – and then ignore them without a thought, slicing icily through red tape with that biting of the lip which could mean trouble. 'Bureaucrats are Philistines,' he would mutter. 'If we can't beat them we need our heads examined.' But he was equally swift at self-deprecation. 'Where shall I sit? My natural place is under the table'; and he would double up with that childlike giggle which sat so strangely with his dignified persona.

His wit was a constant joy, his thoughtful help a revelation, and it was a marvellous surprise to break through the shyness and find that he had vision, enterprise, and a sharply questing mind. He was ever lifting his eyes towards fresh horizons, always anticipating the next surge at the end of the runway. 'Not another holiday?' I said. 'No,' he drawled, 'ethnic research'; and off he went to India or Borneo or Chile.

But for all his travelling it was his greatest delight to return to Mount Stuart. 'The weekend was splendid,' he wrote in April 1992, 'hordes of children and Easter eggs, usually in sticky accretion.' Easter was precious, for by then he was ill and as the months advanced the self-deprecation took on a different tone. 'It seems likely that I shall go for a new sort of treatment said to be successful with rats. Look out for exciting changes of appearance and personal habits.'

The changes were profound as he was tempered by the fire of the cancer. It swept away his reticence and brought an eagerness to share the things he was learning. 'This illness has been a gift, it has taught me so much. You cannot have an experience like this and not be changed *forever*.'

His voice was slightly distorted but brimming with enthusiasm; and with that immaculate grace which sustained him on his long journey forward he spoke of his joy at the love which flowed out to him from family and friends 'There are no words to describe what it means to have people who *care* and are supportive. It is simply wonderful. You have all been fantastic. . .'

He was thrilled by his last visit to America: 'It was just amazing, they were so *positive*. How can I tell you what it is like to know that, even if I die, the *quality* of my life can be good; that is such a relief. . .it makes me feel stronger,' he said in June of 1993.

But in his honest and courageous way he handed down a caveat and sought to bring comfort for his going. 'I do not expect miracles, but the tumour has reduced, so we shall see. But whatever happens I want you all to remember that this has been a gift and I am peaceful.'

BRIEFLY JOHN. . .

I remember an evening in the Fine Arts Society, Bond Street, London, where John was hosting a reception for the Edinburgh Tapestry Company. He moved sharply to avoid champagne spray and was horrified to realise he had split the seam of his jacket. We teased him about buying his suits at Oxfam and it prompted the following note: 'Didn't we have a ripping time? I noticed that you yourself took on a distinct look of Tina Turner and hope your hair was respectable before Apsley House. I have decided I must diet so am now off walking in Udaipur, the world's greatest slimming centre. See you lighter and later.'

His generosity was constant and famously discreet: 'My conscience, one of my weaker muscles, will not permit me to allow the Society to bear the total cost of the supper,' he wrote in 1989, 'so I am enclosing a contribution thereto, herewith. I know you will use it with *utmost* discretion.'

'Sorry I'm late. My skateboard broke down.'

'How *do* you spell Bus Q?'

'It's wonderful that Anthony's into Old Masters. No! Not me, the real thing.'

And at a reception at Buckingham Palace: 'We're going on to the theatre; *The Madness of George III* – probably entirely appropriate!'

David Wemyss

Among the many contributions of the Bute family to the protection of and the interest in Scotland's heritage – the castles and houses, the committees and the listings, etc. etc., we must not forget that remote group of islands, way out beyond the Outer Hebrides, St Kilda.

John never went there until a day not too long before his death. But his father before him, who went there often (in the Bristol Channel pilot cutter *Hirta*), and he himself had much to do with these islands. His father bequeathed them to the National Trust for Scotland, and John, already deeply interested in the Trust at that stage, helped to make sure that this bequest was actually effective.

St Kilda was Scotland's first World Heritage Site, and a most worthy one. 'The spectacular character of the great sea cliffs and stacs with their teeming sea-bird colonies, the many remains of past human settlement and the detailed record of the islands' natural and cultural history, combine to impress all who venture to St Kilda.' John's father saw this clearly, and after the 1930 evacuation of the inhabitants he bought the islands. This was the first step in their conservation.

John had always been kindly disposed to the National Trust for Scotland, following the example of his own father in the Thirties. But he was undoubtedly taking a risk when he accepted the Trust as his tenant in No. 5 Charlotte Square in 1949, well knowing that this tenant was well-nigh bankrupt. A few years later he decided to place even more faith in the Trust when he bequeathed the St Kilda archipelago to his tenant.

John was well aware of the long drawn out discussions within the Council and Executive of the Trust before his father's bequest was formally accepted, with a mixture of gratitude and trepidation. Reasons for hesitation were many and very clear. A distinguished admiral said the anchorage and the navigation were dangerous. A distinguished lawyer said the whole idea was *ultra vires*. But I was among those who were determined that, if it were at all possible, the islands should be accepted by the Trust. The legend is, and it may or may not have a thread of truth in it, that after a Council meeting which was unable to come to a decision, I said, 'Well, we will have to go on discussing it until we do come to a decision to accept.' And indeed, they did so decide.

All this coincided with the Government and the Royal Air Force (later replaced by the Army) deciding that they must have a station on St Kilda to track the fall of the missiles from the new firing range

in South Uist. The intricate exercise of fitting in this Service require-
ment with the Nature Conservancy Council, and preventing the
whole nineteenth-century village being bulldozed for road metal,
was mainly the work of Jamie Stormonth Darling, the Chief Executive of the Trust, who almost singly saw the immense archaeological value of all these structures, disregarded by relevant Government departments.

So Trust ownership and occupation of the islands began, with
cruises and work parties and all the rest. And John, for many years,
with his busy life and his continuous service to the Trust, as well as
to a multitude of other national and local causes, was so occupied
that he never allowed himself time to get in his boat and sail out
and enjoy his father's islands, and to appreciate the kind of life
lived there when his father made his ornithological researches on
Hirta.

When John did eventually sail out on his beloved *King Duck*, it
was perhaps by way of a pilgrimage, since by that time his health
showed signs of failing. It was therefore of deep significance that he
wrote a postcard (not an example from his famous or infamous
collection) to report in his characteristically crisp and lucid way
that he felt very happy, and certain that his father would have been
pleased with the way the Trust in which he had placed *his* trust
had, for nearly forty years, discharged its responsibilities over his
bequest.

It must surely be an inspiration to us all that John achieved that
voyage and sailed away from St Kilda happy and contented that the
Trust, which he had led so well, and for which he had worked so
hard, had not failed his father, nor yet himself.

David Wilson

John Bute was such a splendid and amusing companion that it
would be easy to forget him in one of his most important and
influential roles, as chairman of committee. Like most academics,
much of my life has been spent in indulging that peculiarly British
habit of sitting on committees. I have no hesitation in saying that
John was the best chairman I have ever sat under – and so, without exception, would all the members of the Museum Advisory

Group set up by the Secretary of State for Scotland to oversee the transformation of the Royal Museum of Scotland and the National Museum of Antiquities of Scotland into a single institution.

For nearly six months we met periodically in a windowless and practically airless room in new St Andrew's House for a day's hard work; the only respite from which was a grisly, wineless meal in the canteen of that misbegotten monstrosity. John with boundless good humour and tart comment got us to rise above our surroundings and led us to produce a report which was accepted in its entirety (if rather grudgingly) by the Secretary of State and produced John's greatest monument – the National Museum of Scotland, with a new board of Trustees (of which he remained Chairman until his death) and a new building in Chambers Street which he personally shoehorned out of a far-from-generous Government.

We had a splendid time. John was introduced to the more arcane aspects of museum life. A visit to Biggar gasworks was a high point, a low point perhaps the discovery that the Museum of Antiquities had a barracks full of old ploughs, all lovingly cared for and inventoried. We interviewed the staff, took evidence from civil servants, were browbeaten by hopeful amenity bodies and read submissions from the west of Scotland. We even went to Wales! John was imperturbable, tactful, occasionally blasphemous, and welded the committee into a body of friends who, until his death, met annually to dine and celebrate victory over the philistine hordes of the Scottish Office.

Susan Wraight

I was introduced to Lord Bute by Amanda Game of the Scottish Gallery, after she had discussed with him a project for the construction of a rather grand bed for Mount Stuart's Horoscope Room. This had originally been a sitting room, panelled with finely carved walnut, and named for the horoscope of the 3rd Marquess of Bute, which adorns the richly decorated ceiling. It was now a bedroom, and someone was needed to carve three finials – two for the bedposts at the foot of the bed, and one for the top of the canopy – and Lord Bute, who had already bought two of my netsuke, wrote to ask if I would accept this commission.

My first meeting with him took place in 1991 at Queen Anne's Gate in London. Lord Bute explained that whilst the work he required had to sit well within the Victorian character of the house and would therefore need a traditional base, he was not looking for slavish reproduction, but rather for a lively re-interpretation of the themes within the room. This laudable approach I later found to be consistent across all the projects upon which he had embarked at Mount Stuart. His enthusiasm for the commission, evident pride in what sounded like a truly remarkable house, and the tantalising challenge to produce work that would sit alongside that of William Burges, the architect, and his outstanding craftsmen made the proposal irresistible. I accepted the commission with great relish and was invited to Mount Stuart the following month to see the Horoscope Room for myself.

My first visit to Mount Stuart gave me an impression of Lord Bute that stays with me still, and was confirmed by later acquaintance with him. In all our discussions he paid such close attention to what I had to say about the work in hand that I began to think that mine was the most important project in the house, which it patently could not have been, and this most endearing trait is one I presume everyone who encountered him felt. His humour, always present, and his relaxed manner, made him an easy person with whom to communicate, and yet he was decisive and perceptive, with a quick eye for detail, and these characteristics made him a challenging and rewarding person for whom to work. After viewing the room, and talking to both Lord and Lady Bute, I returned home and wrote a report making suggestions as to possible approaches for the required carvings.

The design process took no little time, involving discussion, models, drawings, amendments – all the usual aspects – and Lord Bute's insistence that there must be some point on the carvings where he could hang his pyjamas. . . .

The final carvings depicted animal musicians, a dominant theme in the panelling around the room, and to unify the figures I chose to represent them as characters from the legend of 'Reynard the Fox', a medieval tale congruent with the gothic references in the surrounding space. At the foot of the bed, Reynard the Fox plays a psaltery, glancing slyly sideways towards Grimbard the Badger, who sits on the opposite post, holding bagpipes and smiling benignly. Above them both, at the top of the canopy, Noble the Lion is being lulled to sleep by their music. What had been a heraldic pose has slipped somewhat, and his head, nodding forward as his eyes close, has a night cap (one of Lord Bute's suggestions, and marked with a marquess's coronet) on the heavy mane. At the sides of the bed, where poles hold back the canopy, there are two masks – one of a crowing rooster to symbolise the morning, and one of an owl, for the dusk.

I hope these carvings resonate with my memories of Lord Bute, and celebrate his wisdom, humour and appreciation of the arts. It was a privilege, for even so short a time, to have known him.

IN JOHN BUTE'S OWN WORDS

THE MUSEUM OF SCOTLAND PROJECT

This is much more than purely a museum venture. It is something which is important to the Community and to our Nation. What we create for Scotland should be something of remark and excellence . . . something of which we can be proud, and which will give joy and satisfaction for generations yet to come.

WORLD WILDLIFE FUND, TROON 20 MAY 1973

It is somewhat inappropriate that I should be addressing you this evening for I am quite sure that all of you will know far more than I about the World Wildlife Fund and the underlying facts that make its success so important.

One has no doubt but that the studies of Doctor Dick Laws, for instance, are as familiar to you as is *The Magic Roundabout* to your children; that the complexities of eco-systems must often preoccupy the conversation of your breakfast tables; that predator chain and peck-order are frequently discussed in your households where, assuredly, wildlife will take precedence over Dolce Vita (which is not quite the same thing).

Modern research techniques place a greater emphasis on the value of original source material than scholars and scientists have tended to do in the past. Thus I would tonight, during my speech which Lady Glenarthur suggests might have a duration of about one hour, like to direct your attention to the significance of some particular, and hitherto unpublished, document of direct relevance to our theme.

This is a story by Beatrice Blotter, prolific authoress in the early 1900s, who more than anyone else has been responsible for a massive injection of sentimentality into a subject that is, fundamentally, a matter of resource management.

I was fortunate enough to discover the manuscript: you are the first – in the world – to be appraised of its contents. The title is: 'The Tale of Clint the Weasel'. It reads:

Once upon a time, there were four little weasels and their names were Flopsie, Mopsie, Short-Arse and Clint.

They lived with their mother in a bunker on the Troon golf course, underneath the roots of a plastic tree.

'Now, you bleeding little perishers,' said old Mrs Weasel (who, if truth be told, was an unmarried mother) on one May morning, 'you may go out into the fields to gather pot, or down the by-pass to collect fag-ends, but on no account should you go into the garden of the Marine Hotel: one of your fathers had an accident there; resulting in his being skewered in an impolite place and subsequently barbecued to a turn to be served up, together with a cheeky little wine, to an unsuspecting Japanese tourist.

'There are many dangers in this permissive world,' she continued, 'and I have to go out, so remember do, as often I have repeated, to be careful of these jovial men who are always playing with their little white balls outside the back door, and to watch out for the traffic – especially Colonel Henderson returning home in the evening and the Terror of Kilkerran on her motorbike, and positively resist entering into conversation with Lord Ballantrae or you are bound to be late for supper.'

Then old Mrs Weasel set out across the golf-course for the chemist's shop where, the unkind might say, had she previously got her shopping priorities different, the size of her family might have nearer accorded with Prince Philip's wishes.

The three older children did her bidding; but Clint ran straight to the Marine Hotel, over a mountain of empties at the back door (not so large, I should think, as it will be after tonight) and proceeded to feast on the rich goodies in the garbage can where, it is sad to relate, he compounded his disobedience by overeating in a manner quite disgusting, with the inevitable result that he soon felt more than somewhat sick; so he went to try an find the Shaw-Stewart car which he knew would contain some Alka-Seltzer.

But, turning the corner, whom should he meet but Lord Black-face! A sight, you will agree, for a young weasel, as yet uninitiated in Ayrshire society, most terrible to behold! The Lord, on his knees for dubious reasons of his own, sprang almost immediately to his hob-nailed feet, giving chase, shouting (in rough translation): 'You fu- fu- funny little weasel, wait till I catch you!'

Clint, dreadfully frightened, and despite the surfeit he had consumed, fled at a good pace and was out-distancing his pursuer when carelessly he slipped on one of Bobby Corbett's discarded *bons mots*. Such was his acceleration that he veritably flew through the air, describing the while three perfect somersaults, to land, to his great surprise, in Lord Ailsa's sporran. Even in his state of panic, he could not help noticing that this sartorial accoutrement bore a marked resemblance to one of his deceased uncles; but what riveted his attention was the portentous implication of the family motto inscribed thereupon: 'Consider the End'.

Now this incident was observed by no one at all, save for one very loyal person passing by with, characteristically, a dolly bird on each arm. He, kind and attentive as always, with sleight of hand and a loud guffaw, plucked Clint from his predicament and threw him into a convenient tool shed, which, could its walls speak, would have their own tale to tell for, to quote a well-known comedian, more goals had been scored there on a Saturday night than during decades of local football matches. But that is beside the point.

Lord David was still in pursuit; Jim Sillars had pronounced that weasels should be nationalised; the local Tory party – all three of them – passed a motion asking the Government to bring back the birch; Sir Fitzroy Maclean went to Yugoslavia and ex-Provost Lambie went to sleep.

You may imagine Clint's exhaustion by now, sobbing his little weasel heart out under a flower pot. Worse, however, was yet to come: shaken by the reverberations of his distressed cries the pot fell around him becoming now a prison rather than a refuge.

At 40,000 feet, Captain Shrubshaw, unaware of the heart-rending drama beneath, was occupied in the nineteenth test flight of Concorde II and with habitual disregard broke the sound barrier over the coastal plain, causing some 3,000 ewes to have spontaneous abortions, seven matrons to jump in their seats getting their heads jammed in the hair driers at Mary Loudon, Lord Glenarthur to choke on his stirrup cup and the flower pot to shatter over Clint's head.

Dazed, confused, exhausted, he sought his way home; wandering about, going tippity-lippity, lippity-tip and so forth, rather slowly (how stupid can you get)?. . .

And I think we may skip the next twenty pages which are full of 'yuck' about the plight of the young, together with psychiatric 'mish-mash' upon which it is too late to dwell. . .

In his wanderings he encountered a plastic gnome clad in colours that would put Carnaby Street to shame. Thinking him first to be Terry Scott in disguise, Clint politely requested his autograph; receiving no response he asked him the way home but the gnome was too busy fishing to help him at all.

Eventually he found his way home where Mother Weasel put him to bed with two tranquillisers and much reasoned advice.

But Flopsie, Mopsie and Short-Arse had gin and canapés for supper and were allowed to sit up late watching television.

That is the end of the manuscript; I hope it will have served to stimulate you to redouble your efforts on behalf of the World Wildlife Fund.

SUBSCRIBERS

Contributors are listed in bold type

Adam & Company
Miss R. M. Aitken
Sir Kenneth Alexander
Tim Ambrose
Dr R. G. W. Anderson
Ian Archibald
John C. Asher
Helen R. Auty
Mrs Stuart B. Avery
Samantha Bain
Dr Jean Balfour, CBE, FRSE, DSC,
    FIC FOR, JP
John Barnett
Normile Elliot Baxter
Mrs Normile Elliot Baxter
The late Duchess of Beaufort
Graham Beck
Robert Begg
John Bellany, CBE, RA
Gordon Benson
HMEH The Prince and Grand
    Master, Fra Andrew Bertie
David Bertie
Peregrine Bertie
Liz and Simon Bonham
Louise Boreham
Lester Borley
Mary Borley
The British Council
Sheila M. Brock
The Hon. James Bruce
Nigel Buchanan
The Bute Museum Trustees
David Roderick Cameron

Sir Ilay Campbell of Succoth, Bt
Hugh Cantlie
Cardiff Castle
Caroline Carrington
Sir James Cayzer
Nigel and Henrietta Cayzer
Deepak Chopra
John Clare
A. Trevor Clark, CBE
David Coombs
The Hon. Robert Corbett
Fr Edward Corbould, OSB
John Cornforth
Lady Cowan
Ronnie Cramond, CBE
Patrick and Barbara Crichton
Major J. D. M. Crichton
    Maitland
Anthony Crichton-Stuart
Alexander Crichton-Stuart
Caroline Crichton Stuart
Cathleen Crichton Stuart
The Lady David Crichton-Stuart
Jack Crichton Stuart
Frances Crichton Stuart
Fredrik Crichton-Stuart
Henry Crichton-Stuart
Hugh Crichton-Stuart
Jane Crichton-Stuart
Marietta Crichton Stuart
Michael Crichton-Stuart
Niall Crichton-Stuart
Sophia Crichton Stuart
William Crichton-Stuart

Lady Cubitt
Cumnock and Doon Valley District
  Council, District Library and
  Museum Service
Caroline Cuthbert
Lady Victoria Cuthbert
June B. Da Costa
The Earl and Countess of Dalkeith
Tam Dalyell
Julian David
John and Coralie Davie
Warren Davis
Ben Dawson
Mrs Edward Denny
The Lord De Ramsey
Mr and Mrs Ian H. Dobinson
Patricia Douglas
Rear Admiral Douglas Dow, CB
Sir Philip Dowson
Maldwin Drummond
Andrew Drysdale
The Marchioness of Dufferin and
  Ava
Freddie Dumfries
Johnny Dumfries
Morrison and Sally Dunbar
James Dunbar-Nasmith
Alastair Dunlop
The Countess of Dunmore
Sir Alastair Dunnett
The Edinburgh Tapestry Company
Dr Raymond Edwards, OBE, LLD
Alun Emlyn-Jones, OBE, JP
Tom Errington
Rory Faber
The late Sir Nicholas Fairbairn
Peregrine Fairfax
Anna Fekete
Alexius Fennick
Georgia Fennick
Benedict and Deirdre Fenwick
Captain and Mrs Andrew Ferguson
Mr and Mrs John R. Findlay, MBE
Mrs E. B. V. Fletcher

Alan and Sandra Forsyth
D. Donald M. Frame, CA
Sir Charles and Lady Fraser
Liz Fraser
Friends of Rothesay Castle
Martin Gardner
Christian Gaze
J. Paul Getty, KBE
John and Patricia Gibbons
Christopher Gibbs
Stephen and Lavinia Gibbs
Dr J. A. Gibson, Chairman, Scottish
  Natural History Library
Jay L. Glaser, MD
The Earl of Glasgow
Michael Goedhuis
The Lord Goold
Bobby Gordon
Sir Alistair and Lady Grant
D. P. J. Grant
Sandy Grant Gordon
John Greenall
Kenneth R. Grimston
The Earl and Countess of
  Haddington
Arthur Hall
Michael Hall
Elizabeth, Duchess of Hamilton
J. Donald M. Hardie, OBE, DL,
  FRSA
Sally Hardie
Marshall J. Harris
Sheriff Principal and Mrs Robert
  Hay
Professor and Mrs D. M. Henderson
Clare Henry
Anthony Hobson
Michael Holloway
John Home-Rigg
Sheriff William Hook, QC
Antony Hornyold
Jocelyn Humfrey
Mrs Alison Hunter
James Hunter Blair

Professor David S. Ingram scd,
  fibiol, frse
Lady Innes
Miranda Iveagh
Dr Peter F. Jack
Richard W. Jenner
Mrs Pat Jolly
Professor Peter Jones
Mr and Mrs Alastair Kennedy
Mrs David Kindersley
Dick Kingzett
Alison Kinnaird
Anna Rose Knatchbull-Hugessen
Colonel T. B. M. Lamb, obe, dl
Sir David Landale, kcvo
Andrew and Jillian Liddell
Norman S. Lindsay
Richard and Elizabeth Lindsey
John D. Lloyd-Morgan
Angela and Jimmy Logan
Fiona and Michael Lowsley-
  Williams
Mark Lowsley-Williams
Miggie Lowsley-Williams
Patrick Lowsley-Williams
Paul Lowsley-Williams
Christopher Lucas, cbe
Ellice McDonald, Jr, cbe
Rosa Laird McDonald, cbe
A. J. Macdonald-Buchanan
Neil G. Macfarlane
Lord and Lady Macfarlane of
  Bearsden
Sir Charles and Lady McGrigor
Mrs Jane Machin
Mrs B. S. Mackie
Ian Maclagan, llb, fsa scot.
Sir Fitzroy Maclean, Bt
Iain L. MacLeod
Very Rev Iain Canon MacMaster
Sir Thomas Macpherson
J. C. T. MacRobert
John McVey
Patricia Mary McVey, ba

The Earl of Mansfield
The Lord Marlesford, dl
Dr Rosalind K. Marshall
Hanne Mason
Ronald J. A. Masters
Henry Meyric Hughes
James and Iris Miller
Margaret Miller
Ronald and Ann Miller
Mrs Carol Mitchell
Hal Moggridge
James J. More
Mr and Mrs James Morris
Alberto Morrocco
John Mott
The Lord Mowbray and Stourton
The Duke of Norfolk
David and Phoebe Orr
Thomas I. Parkinson, Jr
William Paterson
Alex Paulin
Francesca Pelizzoli
Mary Pendreigh
Andrew Percy
Diana Percy
Katherine Percy
Richard Percy
The Earl of Perth
Sheila Pettit
Mrs L. M. Phillips
Jeremy Pilcher
Meredith Pilcher
David and Sue Pirnie
Nigel Pittman
Jane Priestman, obe
Dr and Mrs Derek Pringle
John Ramsay
Dick Reid
Richard and Suzie Reynolds
Anthony Rhodes
R. T. Richardson, obe
John Martin Robinson, fsa
Angela Rodriguez
Jorge Ross

Sir Steven Runciman
Francis Russell
The Saltire Society
Mr and Mrs Alastair Salvesen
Pauline Sargent and the late James
  Sargent
The Earl of Scarbrough
Timothy and Ellen Schroder
Mr and Mrs C. M. Scott
Philippa Scott
Melvin Seiden and Janine Luke
Sir Alexander and Lady Sharp
  Bethune
Houston Shaw-Stewart
Lucinda Shaw-Stewart
The Earl of Shelburne
Billy Shields
Jimmy Shields
Anne and Jim Simpson
Ian N. Skolnick, CA
Robert H. Smith
Dom Alberic Stacpoole, OSB
Reo Stakis
Gavin Stamp
Mike Stanfield
David and Annabel Stapleton
Mr and Mrs Robert Steedman
Jeannie Calder Stewart
Mr and Mrs George M. Stewart
Blair and Mary Stewart-Wilson
Jamie Stormonth Darling
Mary Stormonth Darling
Lord Strathcona and Mount
  Royal
Jeanette Sturgeon and the late Ezek.
  Sturgeon

Flora Stuart
Sir John and Lady Swinton
Mrs Rosalind J. Taylor, B.ARCH,
  FSA SCOT., RIBA, ARIAS
J. A. and M. B. Thomas
Kate Thornton
Stewart Tod
Sir Simon Towneley, KCVO, JP
George C. Train
Professor Tony Travis
Turf Club
University of Strathclyde
Katie van der Werff
Rosemary Verey
Mr Richard and the Hon. Mrs
  Vernon
Sir Humphry and the Hon. Lady
  Wakefield
David Walker
Diane A. Walker
Professor Andrew Walls, OBE
James Wardrop
Diana Warwick
Kay Watt
Janet Wears
Stephen Weeks
The Earl of Wemyss and March
Sir Anthony and Lady Wheeler
Sir Alwyn and Lady Williams
Matthew Williams
Mr and Mrs Michael Whitbread
W. M. Whiteside
Lady Willoughby de Eresby
Sir David Wilson
Ivor and Caroline Windsor
Susan Wraight